Hello, Old Friend

A Resource Guide
For Career Development

Mike Jones

ISBN: 1491044179

ISBN 13: 9781491044179

Library of Congress Control Number: 2013913672
CreateSpace Independent Publishing Platform
North Charleston, South Carolina

To Linda Holt for her tireless dedication, leading by example and her selfless approach to life. She taught me much and will be missed. She will always be remembered.

Contents

Foreword

"All our dreams can come true...
if we have the courage to pursue them."

~Walt Disney

My name is Brian Leach and I am the co-founder and CEO of Unboxed Technology. Routinely I get asked, "How does it feel to own your own business?" My typical response is that it's exciting, crazy, and scary all in one breath! To this day I chalk up my decision to become an entrepreneur to a series of God Winks and life intersections that were well beyond my control.

I spent twenty years of my career with a Fortune 500 retailer living the corporate dream. Over that period I advanced from a front-line sales representative to a vice president and officer leading the development of an innovative retail concept. During that twenty-year period I married my beautiful wife, Dawn, we were blessed with three wonderful children and we moved on three different occasions to propel my career. It was the ultimate sacrifice, and I had it all figured out. I had accumulated a solid company stock portfolio, had a job contract to cover any risk, and a dream job. That is, until January 16th, 2009. That wonderful company that I loved so dearly filed for bankruptcy and closed its doors within weeks. More than 30,000 wonderful people lost their jobs that day. My company stock portfolio was gone, my contract was essentially invalid, and my dream job was just a memory. I was in shock. My world was rocked and I had no plan for a transition. One of my last memories of that job is sitting in a conference room with my team updating our resumes. I packed my bags, and, with two weeks pay, started out on a new journey.

As bad as this sounds, I only had one regret. I regret that I didn't spend any time marketing myself over that twenty-year period. I had ignored many new opportunities along the way and I did a really bad job of maintaining an active network. I can only recall going on two interviews during that entire twenty-year period.

What a humbling and sobering experience that was. I can honestly say it's one of the best things that ever happened to me because today I have the honor of leading a rapidly growing software development company that I co-founded. We have been blessed with amazing clients and a team who is sharing the dream. It didn't start out that way, however. I spent six months fine-tuning my resume, refining my story, and applying for countless job openings. I even had a job offer to become the COO of a niche retailer but that offer was rescinded prior to my start date! When I reflect now, I realize that each of these events was a series of intersections. Those intersections were not coincidences. Something more substantial was at play, and when I slowed down and looked closely, I was able to begin pulling the pieces together.

Throughout my journey from unemployed to entrepreneur, I had many intersections with Mike Jones. I first met Mike when he was an executive with my previous company.

Mike had developed a reputation of being a great coach, and was adept at challenging people who were contemplating a job change or who were in a career transition. I reached out to Mike and he agreed to meet with me over coffee one morning. He spent endless hours, over a period of many months, working with me to apply pieces of the framework that you're getting ready to explore in this book. To this day my business partner, Dave, and I cite those intersections with Mike as pivotal. I'm not sure we would have pursued the dreams of becoming entrepreneurs without Mike's influence and the incredible support of our families. While starting a new company has been hard work, I'm so grateful to have the opportunity to get up each day and work on something I love to do!

Let me share a few thoughts as you begin to read this book:

- Mike wrote this book not to become a best-selling author; he's the most selfless person you'll ever meet. A number of people Mike has helped over the years have come to realize his gift of helping others and encouraged him to share it more broadly.

This book contains a framework, stories, and resources you can use to shape or reshape your career.
- Be prepared to work hard and not discount self-reflection along your journey.
- Believe in yourself! If you believe in yourself, it's amazing what you can accomplish!

Good luck, and may your journey be as fruitful as mine! Plan to say "hello" to a new you!

Brian Leach
CEO, Unboxed Technology

Who am I?

"You recognize a survivor when you see one.
You recognize a fighter when you see one."

~ Elizabeth Edwards

To understand where someone is today, you have to first understand where he or she came from. When I look into the mirror of my life's journey, I see the reflection of a survivor, a fighter. Nothing came easy for me. There was no instruction manual accompanying my life. My father left when I was four. My mother worked evenings six nights a week. I didn't know an extended family. We didn't own a car or have much in the way of material things. This made me appreciate the little things I saved up for by collecting and selling soda bottles for two cents apiece. I walked most places I wanted to go, or, because it was safe back then, I'd "hitch" a ride with a stranger. Selfishly and silently, I prayed each night that God wouldn't take my mom away, but would protect her because she was all that I had.

Observing the lives of my friends, I raised myself, doing the best I could. I remember like it was yesterday, playing games outdoors from sunrise to sunset. My neighborhood friends and I played them all - football, basketball, baseball - it didn't matter. Even back then observing behaviors, encouraging teammates and being supportive were becoming my professions.

I did receive a gift in my high school years. I was admitted to an all-boys military high school. During that time I felt a spiritual hand on my shoulder. I appreciated the much needed discipline and leadership that were provided. In my senior year I was promoted to the rank of captain, and I got my first taste of leadership.

I couldn't afford college, and didn't know what I wanted to do even if money weren't an issue. Instead I went immediately to work on my first job and attended school in the evenings.

I lacked self-confidence and I lived with the sense that I was never 'good enough'. I did learn what I could control: my own personal work ethic. I made it a point to arrive at work and to meetings early. I volunteered for assignments and never complained about anything. Within six months on my first job I was promoted to supervisor. I relentlessly studied people and behaviors. Starting at an entry level of the organization afforded me the opportunity to see others struggle and fight for advancement. I found I could outwork others, particularly those who felt deserving and superior.

Studying people, their personalities, their values and their behaviors became a passion of mine. I developed sharper listening skills and a deeper empathy for others. I worked hard, I fought, I listened and I led. I motivated others around me to follow my lead; find their own God-given talents. This was my gift, but I didn't know it yet.

I continued to rise in the employment ranks and tackled my demons of low self-esteem. Instead of staring at my shoes when volunteer opportunities came along, I stared fear in the eye and battled back by raising my hand for the job. Over time I taught, I led, I gave lectures, presentations and speeches. I got involved with numerous charity organizations beginning as a volunteer, then a committee member and became a board member. I grew in many ways, but I never forgot where I started. I now take nothing for granted and look to help others as a calling in my life. Evolving into a servant leader has deep humble roots within me.

I've led groups, departments, divisions and also companies, large and small, for-profit and not-for-profit. I've hired, nurtured and lost many people along the way. I have a love for life's intersections. I've survived a serious health scare, which has served to intensify my focus on my attitude of gratitude.

I've developed points of view, innovative strategies, and a strong contrarian determination. I look at life from all sides. I work hard to understand people and their plights. I always strive to be honest and candid, yet caring. I've been told many, many times that I am really good at what I do, and it's why people seek my advice and counsel. I discovered my talent and now I seek to help others find theirs.

This leg of my journey has wiped out my timidity and gifted me with courage to relate to and teach others. For my clients, I must solve their problems. I have to make each session and interaction so meaningful they will want to continue.

Over the years, I realized the biggest problem facing those in need of a job is a strong cloak of desperation coupled with scant preparation. From the hundreds of networking interviews I have performed, I have applied my increased learning and knowledge to build out a framework to teach from. It is my hope that others on this path might benefit from the experienced footprints in the sand of those who walked before them.

There is no panacea; only hard work and determination. But without some framework, you will not be at your absolute best. It's serendipitous in a sense that I offer something that I didn't have when I was coming along. I sure could have benefited from it.

Because I felt alone for so many years in my struggles, I don't want you to feel alone in your journey during this difficult time in your life. Whether you are just starting your career, in mid-career flux or trying to reenter the workforce, there is much between these covers to provide you sustenance.

Allow me to share some of my stories that have helped others - others who may have felt exactly what you are feeling now. I hope you will find that you are not alone, but that many of us have walked this path before you. In my own personal way, I say to you, "Hello, Old Friend."

"The two most important days of your life are the day you are born and the day you find out why."

~ Mark Twain

Introduction - My Why

It has taken me nearly 40 years in business to begin to fully understand my personal "Why". Simon Sinek, author of **Start With Why**, *explains that "people don't buy* **What** *you do, they buy* **Why** *you do it." When you start with the what, you are defining a commodity. I refuse to be a commodity. After working with hundreds of individuals who have been on a networking journey trying to find their next career challenge, I discovered "why" I'm so committed to assisting others. Here is my Why:*

> *"I wish to inspire others to find what inspires them.*
> *I want to sell them a dream of a better tomorrow."*

Whether I am counseling a friend, a stranger, a client or an associate, I push, probe and challenge in an attempt to peel away nebulous responses to get at the heart of their bliss and their wants from life. I will often play the contrarian to see if I can change their stance or position, and, if I am successful, I quickly take the side they just departed from and begin anew!

Joseph Campbell, teacher, author and expert in mythology, stressed that each of us should "follow our bliss...when you're on a journey, and the end keeps getting further and further away, then you realize that the real end is the journey." I stress to everyone I network with that they should work hard to identify those things they like to do that feels almost criminal to be paid for. Remember as kids when we would hear professional ballplayers say, "I'd play for free, I love the game so much!"? When one genuinely enjoys what they do, when they feel they are playing to their strengths, it doesn't feel like work. We should all be so fortunate to capture such a career.

If you want a convincing example of this, bliss and pursuit of passion, rent the film documentary, Jiro Dreams of Sushi. *A good friend, Sydney, introduced me to this work. We met recently to discuss the outline of my book.*

While concentrating on bliss, practice and focus, she stressed to me to check out the film for a striking example of bliss and practice. This 2011 film, directed by David Gelb, follows Jiro Ono, an 85-year-old sushi master and owner of Sukiyabashi Jiro, a Michelin three-star restaurant in Japan, on his life journey to perfect the art of sushi. In his introduction Jiro says, "Once you decide on your occupation, you must immerse yourself in your work, you have to fall in love with your work, never complain about your job, you must dedicate your life to mastering your skill. That's the secret of success and is the key to being regarded honorably." How many of us can attest to this philosophy? Moreover, how many people do you know who live this devotion?

In their book, Now, Discover Your Strengths, *Marcus Buckingham and Donald Clifton cite a study completed by the Gallup Organization in which they asked this one question of more than 1.7 million employees working in 101 companies from 63 countries: At work do you have the opportunity to do what you do best every day? The response? Globally, only 20 percent of surveyed employees working in large organizations felt that their strengths were in play every day! This astounds me, as we are entirely free to choose and pursue our career passions.*

Additionally, from my earliest memories of my career, I recall pledging to never turn someone down who wished to network with me. Why? I felt that we are all one step away from being that person who needs a helping hand, or needs to engage with someone to encourage them, listen to them, challenge them, and in the end, broker introductions. I hoped that good karma would follow me.

In recent years and certainly since the economic collapse of 2008, my networking time has expanded exponentially. At its busiest, my partners and I were speaking with 20 unemployed individuals per week. As local companies fell into bankruptcy, the number grew and the pace hurried for those looking for work. I remember at the onset of these times, one worry that plagued many in this large group was, "How is this blemish going to look on my resume?" In hindsight we now know it held little effect as too many good, strong and capable individuals were competing for fewer and fewer openings, creating lengthy gaps in their employment record. It became relatively easy to address as so many others had the same blemish on their resumes, too.

I recall a networking moment when I cautioned an individual that he was emitting a strong plea of desperation in his conversation and he blurted out, "But I am desperate!" I saw this type of stress regularly as firms quickly moved to downsize staff and shed excess weight. This was perhaps necessary for the firm's survival, but not a desired outcome for the employee.

Out of my quest to help others, I developed a pretty good framework to assist those in need of career development. This framework has been truly tested with many individuals since 2008. I now hope to help you – whether you are just embarking on your career, in the middle of a career crisis or just want that little nudge to ensure you are still in pursuit of your bliss.

*I hope you enjoy this collection of musings and personal insights, now constructed as a career resource guide just for you! I'm willing to bet you will find something of value and I encourage you to pick up a highlighter and make this a more personal journey. My wish is that with this book you will find a good companion. Now is the time to introduce yourself to the person in the mirror. Claim your identity, your talents, your passions and whisper the words – **Hello, Old Friend**.*

Enjoy!

A Time of Crisis

"Every little thing counts in a crisis."

~ *Jawaharlal Nehru*

The exact date is unimportant, but the call that came to my office in early 2008 was a defining moment. But who knew? Linda, who manages our front reception area, forwarded Doug's call to my office. "Mike, there has been a large number of recent layoffs and I would appreciate it if you would help some of these folks network and find employment." Doug is a friend who happens to have a lead role with a large outplacement firm. His firm is retained by a number of mid-to-large employers who provide outplacement services to their displaced associates as a component of their severance package. What neither of us knew at that time was just how deep the wave of unemployment would be felt locally, regionally and on a national level.

I know our firm has met with and coached hundreds of individuals since that fateful day. Who can really say when it officially started? After all, we had been meeting regularly with individuals who were examining their careers well before the recent economic recession. But it had certainly not been in such cataclysmic proportions.

It began to feel a little like a MASH triage effort. We prioritized those who most needed our assistance to the best of our abilities. What we saw was consistent – they were each hurting, they needed to release some pent-up emotions and they wanted to return to the battle, the job market, as quickly as possible.

As the years progressed, I found myself delivering much of the same material to just about every individual I met with. The topics included:

- Crafting and owning your story
- Critiquing and improving your resume
- Building your confidence
- Expanding your network
- Developing your personal marketing plan
- Coaching for the interview (preparation, planning, role-playing)
- Evaluating corporate alternatives (consulting, entrepreneurship, non-profit)

Many tips have been feathered into my talk along with countless stories that are a part of my past, and also stories accumulated from others during this lengthy period of corporate downsizing.

While I am hopeful we are recovering from the worst of these times, there certainly will be future events that will require this material again and again.

Life is a Series of Intersections

"Always show more kindness than seems necessary, because the person receiving it needs it more than you will ever know."

~ Unknown

Have you ever felt when you're talking with someone that there was more than a coincidence at play? Maybe you suspected that there was a reason, a sense of purpose for this discussion to occur, more than just a random sequence of events. I know I have. I looked for the connection, as "random" was eliminated from my thought process. There was a reason –and invariably it became clear. I listened more intently. At some point I began coining the phrase, 'life is a series of intersections'. What we do at those intersections is where magic can occur. These intersections also shape and define us.

A perfect example of this occurred just before the close of 2011. I was meeting someone for the first time who was new to our community. Fred had been introduced to me through a mutual friend. He was having a difficult time finding a meaningful work challenge. He had done a tremendous job of attending breakfast meetings, civic gatherings and establishing his professional network. But having relocated from Florida and knowing no one in our area, his attempt to find his bliss and to begin making a difference was stressful. As I learned more of Fred's background and found his passion for process improvement and workflow engineering, I discovered a personal connection. Just days earlier I had uncovered a need that a client had for a major functional and organizational assessment. The timing of our 'intersection' couldn't have been more aligned and purposeful. We spoke for a couple of hours. The engine of possibilities and meaning roared! I invited Fred to a company gathering I was hosting so he could meet others in our work family. We continued vetting each other. Fast forwarding twelve months, the client has accepted him as one of their own, a high compliment. Fred has introduced much positive change and found additional ways to add value.

Another meaningful intersection occurred in the spring of 2010. I was meeting with a good friend, Brian. Brian had just exited his employer, a company that was in the final stages of bankruptcy. He was exploring what would be his next pursuit. As we spoke I found him to be bifurcated. On one hand he was feeling the stress of finding a new job in order to continue caring for his family. On the other hand, he was being tempted with the possibility of embarking on a business startup. He had established quite an innovative muscle along with a deep confidence at deploying technology within retail in a very unique and exciting fashion. It was a blue ocean opportunity. We debated the pros and cons of each choice. I stressed that whatever his decision, he needed to own it and not look back. No "would-a, could-a or should-a". He needed to be resolute once he made his decision.

As we fast-forward three years, Brian is the CEO of a successful, rapidly growing company which one frequently recognizes as a top emerging company. He has been an expanding tenant in our office building, having regular access to counsel and advice. I remember early on as Brian was trying to capture his story, the essence of his corporate being. He was not convincing and his efforts rang with doubt. For two reasons I invited many friends, seasoned business executives with varying backgrounds and perspectives, to meet with Brian individually. This group was comprised of ex-CEO's, equity analysts, effective sales leaders, private investors, bankers and an assortment of other successful people. One outcome of these meetings was that Brian became convincing and strong in his delivery. He owned it. He believed it and his focus became sharp and laser-like. Secondly, each and every person who evaluated Brian's company, vision and business plan, and who listened to him tell his story, became believers. Brian, who grew his company to fifteen employees in the first twenty-four months, will soon add another dozen or so, and has an enviable national client list of who's who in retail.

In summary, at your next networking meeting, when you are at that intersection, stop, listen and search for connections. You may surprise yourself with the paths that open up and how you might drive additional benefit to someone you are just meeting. Don't just check it off the list as an obligation to a friend. Make the intersection an important one. Pay it forward.

"To the world you may be one person, but to one person you may be the world."

~ Bill Wilson

The Framework

"The experiences are so innumerable and varied, that the journey appears to be interminable and the destination is ever out of sight. But the wonder of it is, when at last you reach your destination you find that you had never travelled at all! It was a journey from here to here."

~ Meher Baba

Figure 1

The dictionary defines a framework as "a skeletal support used as a basis for something being constructed." When I consider a framework for career management, a journey that will span the many years and jobs held by any individual, I strive for a repeatable process and demand a strong foundation.

You can apply this framework to your search whether you are just entering the work force for the first time, reentering after a voluntary sabbatical or an involuntary job loss, or you are contemplating a whole new career direction.

The chapters ahead define a framework that begins with Reflection. Reflection will be the foundation upon which you will add the weight of your other layers. Without this strong base for support, the added layers will prove vulnerable and ultimately too weak to properly serve your needs.

As its name implies, Reflection is an intense and careful consideration, a fixation of thoughts on something. Within the confines of this book, Reflection is your total immersion into a self-examination and introspection. It will require complete honesty, humility, and self-understanding. Your desired outcome is to arrive at the real You!

Maybe now you can better understand why I stress its importance as your personal foundation. I cannot emphasize enough the importance of patience and honesty as you explore inwardly to discover your core.

Within the section on Reflection, you will find chapters pertaining to your inner being (You in the Mirror, Confidence), and your inner desires and conflicts (Abundance and Gratitude, Desperation and Worry, Personal Values, Dead-End Jobs, The Grass Isn't Always Greener). I have also included a chapter on Recommended Reading to assist you in your journey of self-discovery. At the end of each of these chapters, your call to action is going to be contemplation and deep, personal reflection, aided by a chapter worksheet to stimulate your thinking. Upon completion of the entire section on Reflection, you will have formed an accurate self-image. This is your foundation. If you have not fully derived an accurate and complete picture, I strongly urge you to return to the beginning of this section and begin anew. Done well, this section will be very satisfying, informative and revealing. It will provide you with the sturdiest of foundations on which to build.

Following Reflection, you will move to the Preparation section of the framework. Within this section the chapters focus on crafting and telling your story, expanding your network, improving your resume and pursuing practice with a relentless mindset. There are a number of action items within these chapters and a worksheet at the conclusion of each that will serve to engage you to make this journey more real and personal. As NBA Basketball phenom, LeBron James, was recently quoted, "When you practice something over and over, it's just second nature to you."

The final section of the framework is Execution. This is where all your reflection and preparation leads to tighter execution. How hard you work in Reflection and Preparation will determine how close you are to flawless execution. The chapters contained within this section detail the job interview. We'll discuss interview coaching, the actual interview itself (The Dreaded Interview) and proper follow-up and next steps.

The framework is a collection and compression of a number of proven techniques and practices. It should not be viewed as a once-and-done series of activities. I urge you to rethink job analysis and career planning as an ongoing process, something requiring a regular rhythm and cadence in your professional career. Always remember to revisit the Reflection section of the framework to validate your priorities and desires for that next job. For instance, when you move in your career from the stage of wealth creation to wealth preservation, your priorities will shift, as will your motivators, and ultimately your desires for personal enrichment. Also, as Sigmund Freud describes in the Pleasure principle, human behavior is motivated by two things – seeking pleasure and avoiding pain. Successful people focus on the pleasurable outcome (increased responsibility, promotion, physical fitness, nutrition and ideal weight, etc.,) rather than the painful process (hard work, extra hours, volunteering for assignments, pain from exercising or dieting, and other personal sacrifices). Apply this in your personal reflection.

The framework for the Career Planning Model is represented at the beginning of this chapter (see Figure 1). This depiction will enable you to better understand the endless flow of the model; the end presents a new beginning.

Let's now move into the first section, Reflection. Remember, this is where you find yourself, gain your confidence and begin preparing for the journey of connecting with your next career challenge. Focus on the pleasurable outcome – The Real You - not the pain associated with the process. I'll warn you that this is hard work, but when done right, the result will be a strong and solid foundation. Shall we begin?

1.Reflection

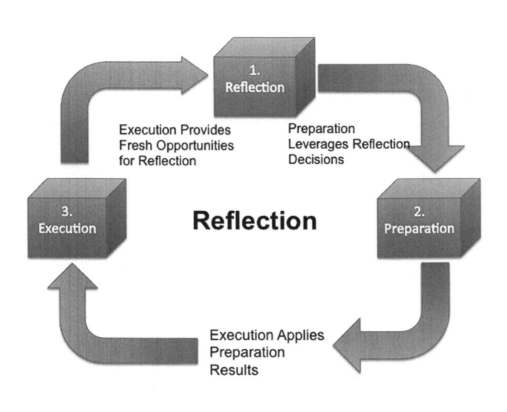

Abundance and Gratitude

"To live a pure unselfish life, one must count nothing
as one's own in the midst of abundance."

~BUDDHA

If you will take a few moments in this period of self-reflection to
consider your insatiable appetite for "adding things" in your life, you
will realize the essence of the theory of abundance. We live in a world
of instant gratification and "not enough". We regularly complain of
not enough time or not enough money or not enough friends or not
enough caring. Whether it's physical, financial, relational, mental or
spiritual, we find the time to covet more. We selfishly hold on to what
we have accumulated, thinking that one day we will have enough. If
we're honest with ourselves, we know that we will probably never
reach that day. This relentless chasing attitude and behavior restricts
us from enjoying what we should be grateful for.

The adage, 'less is more', comes to mind as we try to eliminate com-
plications from our lives, remove complexity, and strive to reduce the
yearning for even more. If we're not careful, this want for more will
drive a downward and negative spiral that can become overwhelming
and unbearable. Look no further than the explosive use of our natural
resources as an example of our want for more. We can't seem to get
enough.

Timberlee, a successful insurance executive and good friend, met with me recently and offered a challenging take on this subject. "Sometimes the 'want for more' can drive reaching and exceeding! It is a fine line and I totally understand your point, but there can be a benefit to wanting more as a motivator, even when you are in transition." I certainly appreciate this perspective, but I worry that our pursuit for more blinds us from taking requisite time to "smell the roses," and to be grateful for who we are, those we have assisted and all we have accomplished.

I've been meeting with a local executive for the past eighteen months offering guidance, direction and encouragement. At a recent encounter he began expressing a need for a job change. "I've been in this role for nearly five years," he stated. "I need a job offering me more total compensation. Due to the tough economy, bonuses have been non-existent and salary increases have been minimal. I'm not accumulating the wealth I had hoped I would." This conversation strikes the abundance chord square on. He has attained a lifestyle he enjoys and wishes to protect and wants to add to. What's been missing over our time together is conversation describing his gratefulness. Surely he has amassed much (more than material wealth) to express gratitude for. He is so sharply focused that he's missing out on the world around him. It reminds me of an old familiar refrain: "He who dies with the most toys wins." I think the real saying should be: "*He who dies with the most toys – still dies.*"

I think it's time we focus on all we have to be thankful for. Are we living *life* abundantly? Having survived a quadruple heart bypass in 2007, I am indeed thankful for what I have and what could have been gone in just the blink of an eye. Be sure to know this: while your desire is for more, there are those around you who want what you have! That's a deep and provocative thought… You want more, but others want what you've obtained. Please reflect on that. And know this, too: once you attain more, your appetite will increase for even more! That's not a phenomenon, but human tendency and conditioning. Once we arrive at a new plateau, we aim a bit higher.

Alter your outlook as necessary. Is the glass half full, or is it half empty? Do you want more, or are you happy with what you have? Gratitude is what is poured into the glass to make it half full. Don't just be grateful for what you have, but also for who you are. The single greatest thing you can do right now to change your life would be to start being grateful for what you already have and who you are. Relax your competitive spirit. Grateful thinking is also associated with increased levels of energy, optimism, and empathy.

> "When you are grateful, fear disappears and abundance appears"

~Anthony Robbins

You might be asking yourself how you can feel grateful when you're in the midst of a job change and feeling all the pressures that accompany that life event. Don't play the victim. Accept the accountability for all that is going on in your life. You own the circumstances and events in your life. Period. No further discussion warranted. This awareness and understanding will allow you to choose your state of mind. Will you concentrate more fully and completely on the things that are right in your life, or dwell on the things gone wrong? The choice is yours and yours alone. While you're reflecting on this, consider that you attract what you feel. Once you are able to focus more positively, with more gratitude for what surrounds you, you will find that the world provides more abundance. More positives will enter your vision and awareness. Just as when more negative thoughts and events enter your mind, the more negative, wanting and demanding you become. When you are down or mad at yourself, when you choose to be upset, and even when you feel fear and anxiety, what vibes, energy and feelings are you projecting? Own up to the fact that you are in charge of you! Decide right now to dispel both negative thoughts and the desire for more of everything. Commit to it...believe it...own it.

Challenge: Try to go an entire day from sunrise to bedtime being grateful and thinking only positive thoughts. The challenge is not if you can do it, but how many times you will fail. How long can you last? One hour? Two hours? Less? And when negatives creep into your thoughts, how long does it take you to refocus yourself? This requires total commitment to changing your outlook. You have to want it, my friend. You have to *really* want it.

Along your transformation journey, you will develop a more acute awareness of the times you fail to maintain an attitude of gratitude. Use this awareness to keep yourself focused on being grateful.

While subtle, I want you to be able to distinguish between reacting and responding to events around you. When you are prescribed a drug for an illness or an injury, you measure its benefits by how your body 'responds' to the drug. When we speak of our body's 'reaction' to the drug, we are describing something our body does without conscious thought. Unlike responding, reacting can have a negative effect. Apply this nuance to your language. Think about responding to things around you, and don't react. Use the attitude of gratitude to be more *responsive* in your life overall.

To highlight both response and gratitude through an example, I am reminded of a time I was visiting a local pizza restaurant. I had stopped in to order a take-home pizza for my family, and while I was watching it being prepared, a customer came in wanting to return her pizza. "This pizza isn't completely cooked," she said. The server looked at the pizza, now missing several slices, and responded, "Ma'am, it really is completely cooked. You ordered a supreme pizza with all the fixings. If we cook it any longer the crust will be ruined." The customer replied she wanted her money back. The server looked over at Tony, the owner, who nodded his approval. He apologized that she didn't find the pizza acceptable and refunded the entire purchase. I observed this interaction, but more importantly I observed what occurred when she left. Nothing disparaging was said and no negative emotions were expressed. After a few minutes I felt my attitude of gratitude and positive response kick in. "Tony, you shouldn't have to lose money on that transaction. She got what she ordered. I'm impressed with the way you responded to her problem. You did not debate or argue with her, and when she left, you did not let it disturb you." Tony replied, "I care more that she might return one day and give us another try. I hope she does." I've seen firsthand how other managers 'reacted' in the very same situation, commenting long after the customer had departed that the customer was wrong, etc.

Back in 1990 I attended an executive program organized by the Cambridge Technology Group at MIT. One of the guest lecturers described his process for regular reflection and personal realignment. "My sacred place for reflection is my barn. I have a farm just outside Chicago and it is more than just my home. It is my sanctuary. I return to my barn regularly, but particularly after traveling. It is here that I return to the familiar smells, sights and sensations. I can sit alone and reflect," he told us. He added that his old, beaten and well-travelled briefcase is his steady companion. Inside it he carried things to keep him connected to his home and family. His barn was his quiet and private respite. I remember how he stressed that each of us should find our own space, that private place for reflection and reconnection. Filmmaker George Lucas once said it in a different context, "It's an issue of quieting your mind so you can listen to yourself." Great and sound advice to digest and employ in reflection.

So now it is time for you to find your quiet place, that place away from noise and competitive distractions. No phones, voices, or other interruptions. Use this place to dive deeply inward. Make connections within yourself, applying what others have provided to you as feedback. Is this how others see you or how you see yourself? Are the accolades and tributes paid to you from others on target? Are the transgressions and poor work behaviors and habits on target? Be honest with yourself.

Challenge: Make your first list. Write down all the things you have to be grateful for. What's on your list? How quickly are you able to jot some things down? Don't stop. Keep adding to your list.

Next, list the things you want more of, that there are "not enough" of in your life. Ask yourself these questions. Why do you want more? Are you ok if you don't get more?

From this chapter, I want you to lay the groundwork for personal transformation and improvement. Profess to take control of your life, hold yourself responsible and agree not to play the victim. Be sincerely and eternally grateful for all you have accomplished and for who you are. Challenge yourself to maintain an attitude of gratitude, whisking away negative thoughts and non-productive incidents.

If you've left an employer, think of people who have stuck with you after you've been gone awhile. When I was recovering in the hospital from major surgery, I'll never forget Jim. He was one of my trusted suppliers before I left my previous employer. It's not unusual for those relationships to dissipate and wither away when you have nothing more to offer them professionally. Not Jim. Residing 300 miles away didn't prohibit him from checking on me and contacting other mutual friends, to notify them of my situation. He drove down to see me, we had dinner and we still continue to have regular contact. We push each other even now to be the best we can be. This is the type of friend you want to pull in to your period of reflection. Someone who wants you to be the best you can be. Who's your Jim?

Finally, realize that within this framework, Reflection is the most significant portion of time you will spend, followed by Preparation and Execution. For many it might be as much as a 60-30-10 split, respectively, in time commitment and overall effort. Let's aim to get it right. Without proper reflection you are left wandering in the dark without a light.

Picture yourself mastering these techniques which will help you live a richer, fuller life.

Chapter Worksheet
Abundance and Gratitude

Not enough? What am I chasing?

Is it difficult for me to maintain an attitude of gratitude? Is it difficult for me to redirect my mind back to a positive outlook when negative distractions are presented? Please comment.

Do I by nature, "respond" or "react"? Do I see the difference and does it matter to me?

What am I grateful for?

What do I see as the need for personal transformation?

What is my key takeaway from this chapter?

Desperation and Worry

"When you reach the end of your rope, tie a knot
and hang on."

~ABRAHAM LINCOLN

Even though desperation and worry will surely serve as motivators in times of crisis, they should be kept at bay and strictly managed as you consider the future of your career and contemplate your next opportunity. I recognize this is a most difficult time for you. You are either out of work, considering changing jobs or are about to launch your career with your very first job. All of these scenarios are worrisome and stressful. You need to maintain a clear head and allow that focus to lead your actions as opposed to acting in desperation.

You can't change the past but you can learn from it. Spending recurring time thinking back will become bothersome as you relive the pain of losing your job. An acquaintance I met a little over a year ago, Kevin, lost his job almost two years ago. He remains bitter and angry about that separation even today. He has been unable to let it go completely and move on. He is more guarded and is having trouble trusting his instincts in returning to a similar role or industry. The hurt that has manifested itself within him has become a chief barrier in his ability to filter and navigate fresh opportunities.

At the other end of the spectrum is my good friend, Mark. Mark had been with a successful hedge fund for several years and had increased his responsibilities steadily while there. Due to declining business, Mark was let go. We discussed his new situation over lunch. "I can't thank them enough," he started out. "They invested in me and gave me opportunities to enhance my skills and sharpen my saw in this very tough and competitive environment." Mark is very upbeat, not clinging to the past and has not become a victim to the situation. He has already begun his reflection and is developing his personal marketing plan by applying his lenses and filters to his job search. He is very focused and has identified both companies and contacts of keen interest to him. I believe in Mark and know he will find continued success in his future.

Not only do you need to let go of the past, you need to stay away from dwelling in the future. The future is not guaranteed and is susceptible to shifts and change. As I am into my fourth year as a vegan, I am frequently asked about my nutritional lifestyle. One question that regularly pops up is, "Are you going to do this for the rest of your life?" I smile at this and simply respond, "I am certain I can make it through today. I commit to today and when tomorrow becomes today, I intend to commit to it then." Forever is a daunting challenge and places enormous weight and pressure on us. If we accept that we can control that which is immediately around us, today in this case, we are better apt to be successful.

Worrying about the future is counterproductive and is misplaced energy. Certainly we should try to understand the worst that could happen. Then we can work with that probability and see what we can do to improve our odds. That's planning in its purest form. It gives us something to wrestle to the ground.

Two years ago another acquaintance, John, became so desperate in his job search that his performance became erratic, scattered and unproductive. He was so paralyzed by the fear of not finding a new job that it interfered with his pursuit. He was unable to truly concentrate and reflect. He simply reacted and churned energy, but made little substantive progress. This stagnation led him to emotional despair and even to payday loans to make ends meet. It didn't have to be this way.

My closing message for you is this: let go of the past. It's over. You lived through the pain once and you don't want to return to it. Stop focusing on the distant future and concentrate on the now, today. Know and accept what you see as the worst ahead and build and execute a plan accordingly. Do not allow yourself to run in place. You must make measurable progress and adjust as needed. Fail early and learn fast. Do not play the victim to your life by blaming others. You must own "you" and hold yourself solely accountable for what happens in and around you.

> "If you don't like something, change it. If you can't change it, change your attitude."

> ~Dr. Maya Angelou

Chapter Worksheet
Desperation and Worry

Am I behaving more like Kevin, Mark or John? What personal behaviors do I need to change to move forward productively?

Who owns my attitude?

Whom do I hold accountable for "me" and where I am?

What is my key takeaway from this chapter?

Personal Values

"It's not hard to make decisions when you know
what your values are."

~ROY DISNEY

Brenda is a young and talented nonprofit leader with strong professional ambitions and great potential. We have been friends for a number of years. She emanates an attitude of gratitude, always focusing on the positive. We met one morning over coffee to discuss her recent change in employment and the process she utilized for her search. "I spent a significant amount of time in reflection," she said. "It was really hard work. I was struggling with what my objections were with my old job. Why was I feeling like such an outsider within my own organization?"

As Brenda and I discussed the framework of this book and the power of reflection, we ambled into a discussion of personal values. "That's it!" she exclaimed. "I had recently met with a good mentor and friend who grounded my thinking and urged me to develop a list of things most important to me - those things I wanted from a job. That was quite a challenge."

Think about your own personal priorities and values. To be certain we are consistent in our understanding of values, let me elaborate. Values exist within you; they lead and support your everyday behavior. They are the things you see as important and are what you use to measure your performance in your life. When in synch, life is generally pretty good, but when your actions are not being led or fed by your values, you will feel a void and general discomfort. You will find that values play an important role in the steps that lie ahead.

Values will shift in accordance with your current life circumstances. For example, where do wealth and family rank on your list? As you start your career, wealth might weigh more heavily than family, as you are likely independent and still creating your own identity and reputation. Those might be reversed later in your life, as you start a family and strive for more work/life balance. (Recently, Steve, a good friend, impressed me by saying, "It's really not balance you seek, but work/life 'integration'." A great perspective, Steve.)

My son, Chris, an energy analyst living in Portland, offered, "Young people will sacrifice many values to land their first job. They have little to trade on and to negotiate with. They might not find ultimate happiness, but they did accomplish their goal of finding work and starting their career." I've reflected on that observation many times and realize compromises are sometimes made to solve more pressing priorities.

Some of my friends debate with me whether values really change. Let me be clear to say that your real core values don't actually leave you, but they may shift in flight. Additionally, there are several plateaus of values we all share. They include family values (belonging, respect, traditions, caring), moral values (compassion, community, fairness, duty), spiritual values (love, selflessness, righteousness) and human values (tolerance, diversity, sharing).

To become Freudian for a moment, let me ask you to try to better understand how your values interact with your id (instinctive part of your personality, immediate satisfaction), your ego (your conscious awareness, judgment and tolerance) and your super-ego (pursuit for perfection, your inner critic). The super-ego controls our sense of right, wrong and the assignment of guilt while contradicting the id (which cherishes instant gratification). From the previous chapter on Abundance and Gratitude, you can see how our behavior of 'not enough' feeds our id.

For many people, the easiest place to start when considering your personal values is to recall the times you were happiest and at your best. Think back to the surroundings, the people you were around, the type of challenges and responsibilities you held. What roles or experiences gave your life purpose and raised your spirit? To aid your personal reflection of values, here is a partial list of values (consider supplementing with your own):

Acceptance	Curiosity	Patience
Accessibility	Determination	Passion
Accountability	Direction	Perfection
Accuracy	Discipline	Philanthropy
Achievement	Diversity	Pleasure
Adaptability	Effectiveness	Power
Advancement	Efficiency	Presence
Adventure	Empathy	Pride
Affection	Encouragement	Professionalism
Altruism	Entrepreneurship	Punctuality
Ambition	Ethics	Recognition
Assertiveness	Excellence	Reflection
Assurance	Experience	Reliability
Balance	Fairness	Reputation
Belonging	Family	Respect
Benevolence	Flexibility	Responsibility
Bliss	Friendship	Selflessness
Camaraderie	Fun	Service
Candor	Gratitude	Significance
Challenge	Growth	Sincerity
Change	Harmony	Status
Clarity	Honesty	Structure
Collaboration	Humility	Success
Commitment	Imagination	Support
Community	Independence	Teaching
Compassion	Influence	Team
Competence	Inspiration	Unity
Competiveness	Integrity	Variety
Confidence	Intensity	Vision
Conformity	Kindness	Wealth
Consistency	Leadership	Wisdom
Contribution	Learning	
Control	Loyalty	
Cooperation	Mentoring	
Creativity	Optimism	
Credibility	Partnership	

Let's return to Brenda's story.

"I began my list with twenty values, which wasn't too difficult. Then I had to cut that in half to ten. That proved more of a challenge, but the real challenge was reducing that to my top five.

I knew that getting honest with myself was really important. I had to admit to myself that things like affection and loyalty were in my core needs and values. I had to deal with the fact that although affection as a value made me feel a little on the weak side, it is a value of mine and mine to own. I needed to be in an environment where I felt appreciated and where kindness was practiced. I also had to admit that 'power' made it to my top ten, which again, I spent more time denying than embracing."

The reason this exercise is so difficult is that it forces deep introspection. You must be honest with yourself. Values are not created equal. You mustn't select those that might make you popular or to be someone you wish you could be.

What was eye-opening for Brenda was her top five values were in conflict with her present job. She wasn't being nourished by her job. Her alignment was off. She needed to reaffirm her values.

"I challenged myself. Are these five values my most important? Are they core to who I am?" Brenda validated her values, feeling very strongly that they defined her. She realized a job change was in order. She had been feeling this emptiness for some time and had a hard time defining the cause. She was now able to take action to correct this misalignment. Ask yourself where you are relative to your own personal values and their alignment with your job. Are your values guiding your actions appropriately?

"Identifying our values gives us a better filter for finding our right place, but it also provides an opportunity for self-improvement. I hope to mature in relation to some of my top ten and learn to better embrace them, rather than deny them or feel guilty for having some of them," Brenda concluded.

See the following diagram (Figure 2) to help you in your own quest to determine your top personal values. Bear in mind that this is most challenging and will likely take several iterations before you get to your most comfortable place. Take your time and strive for certainty.

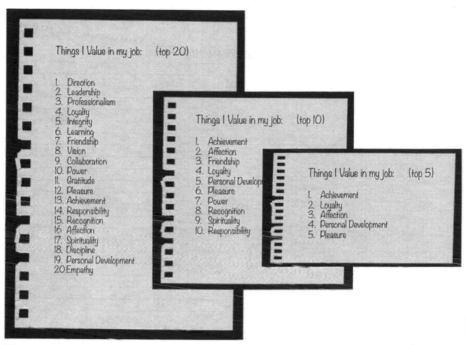

Figure 2

I can attest to the power of values alignment. I am often cited for my enthusiasm and passion. People have asked if I am a preacher. In the sense that I display a passion for an abundance of life, for gratitude, bliss, self-discovery, personal values, networking and for providing service to others, then yes, I am that preacher. When you believe in something with all your being (values) and you are aligned with your life's work, then something magical is resident and beams forth readily. My top 5 personal values are illustrated on Figure 3.

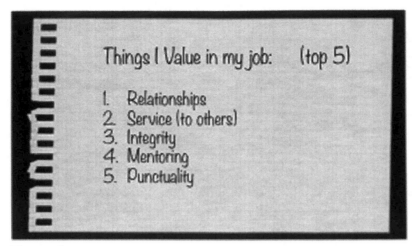

Things I Value in my job: (top 5)

1. Relationships
2. Service (to others)
3. Integrity
4. Mentoring
5. Punctuality

Figure 3

Many of you might be surprised to see punctuality as one of my five key values. I can assure you, it has a strong presence in my life.

In 1991 I had accompanied my management team to our Chicago office for a series of key strategic meetings. On the evening we arrived, our combined teams had dinner and then went downtown to Rush Street for drinks and continued team bonding. We found our way back to the hotel around 4:30 in the morning. Just a few short hours later, as we marshaled ourselves for the walk from the hotel to the office, it became apparent we were going to be cutting it close for our appointed 8:00 a.m. start. Even so, we were committed to walking as one collective unit.

When we arrived at the conference room, just seconds before the appointed hour, we were met in the doorway by Alan, our CEO. His stern look accompanied his only remark to us all, "Do you understand Lombardi time?" Yes I do, Alan. Yes, I do. (Lombardi time is arriving 10-15 minutes earlier than the set meeting time.) That might be my only transgression related to punctuality in my entire career. I make it a priority to be present at my commitments well before the required time. A saying that plays in my mind is, 'never reward those who are late by waiting'. I believe all who know me would confirm these as my values, and as such, I love what I do.

If you are not feeling one hundred percent connected to your job, if you sense something is missing, check your values alignment. If you are well aligned, then your passion, behavior and drive will be obvious to all.

Author James Patterson sketched a wonderful reflective passage in his book, *Suzanne's Diary to Nicholas*:

"Imagine life as a game in which you are juggling some five balls in the air. The balls are called work, family, health, friends and integrity. And you're keeping all of them in the air. But one day you finally come to understand that work is a rubber ball. If you drop it, it will bounce back. But the other four balls – family, health, friends and integrity – are made of glass. If you drop one of these, they will be irrevocably scuffed, nicked, perhaps even shattered. And once you truly understand the lesson of the five balls, you will have the beginnings of balance in your life."

I have found that having balance that includes personal values in your life is critical to overall bliss.

Chapter Worksheet
Personal Values

Is my current job or job desire aligned with my personal values?

What are my top 20 values? Top 10 values? Top 5 values?

Which value is most important to me?

What is my key takeaway from this chapter?

Dead-End Jobs

"The highest reward for a person's toil is not what
they get for it, but what they become by it."

~JOHN RUSKIN

Throughout my career I have frequently encountered individuals who were dissatisfied with their jobs. I find this quite interesting, yet puzzling, since we are employed by our own free choice. Even many who lost their jobs during the most recent economic decline will attest they were not happy; they were not fulfilled.

Karl Lagerfeld, the creative director of Chanel and Fendi, said once, "If you do something that you love, you won't need to force yourself to do it." Is this the debate you're having with yourself right now?

Mellody Hobson, president of Ariel Investments, was quoted saying, "Survivors rescue themselves – they never point fingers, or wait for someone else to rescue them." It's time to look closely at the reflection in your mirror. Who's going to rescue your career, if not you?

I had lunch recently with Krista. I had assisted Krista in her networking efforts to find a new job. In her most recent position there was mutual understanding that neither she nor her employer was satisfied. I had encouraged her to confront the situation. Bad news isn't like wine. It doesn't improve with age. I sensed both parties felt relief and some liberation after this discussion. A satisfying transition plan was negotiated and both parties parted on friendly terms. Now one week into her new role, Krista said that little things she once took for granted have become magnified and have reverberated their importance. For instance, the CEO walked four floors on January 2 extolling the New Year and engaging with staff on their holiday happenings. She was given a tour through the company and introduced to all employees. She was taken to lunch on her first day and quizzed on her interests and career motivations. The smiles, engagement and camaraderie now a part of her new position have been uplifting and serve as a steady stream of motivation. She feels whole, one with purpose and needed. She says there is a strong team presence regularly displayed, something she realized she yearned for when it wasn't evident previously. Let me remind you that we spend the majority of our waking hours at work. We should strive to enjoy it!

Brian, another successful business owner whom I mentioned earlier, asked his associates what makes the company special and why they have elected to stay so committed to the firm. An overwhelming response was, "We know we have each other's back." No one will allow the other to fail. They will drop what they are doing if it appears a fellow associate needs help meeting an approaching deadline. That strong sense of team had formed an adhesive that is bonding them tightly together.

More and more companies have taken steps to measure employee engagement, but not many of those have used the respondent feedback to develop action plans to continually improve the organization. I'm working with a client now whose CEO said to me, "We've asked the employees twice for their feedback. They've given it to us each time and each time we've done absolutely nothing with it." We are now working on an action plan, at his request, to reengage the workforce and re-instill confidence in the leadership team.

Two of the most often asked personnel questions plaguing managers are: Why do employees leave? What motivates employees to stay?

If you are in a dead-end job, a job in which there is little or no chance of progressing or achieving greater responsibility, what has compelled you to remain there? There are countless annual surveys that evaluate job satisfaction. Here is the usual list of motivating factors governing employee retention:

- Job content (interesting work)
- Recognition and appreciation for contributions
- Promotion and growth potential

- Development & training
- Loyalty to employees
- Trust in the organization
- Feeling connected to the mission and objectives of the business
- Good working conditions
- Job security
- Compensation (pay and benefits)
- Corporate culture

On the reverse front, below is the list of reasons associates often cite that lead them to terminate their employment:

- Heavy workload
- Long hours (work/life balance)
- Lack of opportunities for growth and advancement
- Unrealistic demands
- Lack of fit
- Lack of empowerment
- Lack of leadership / communication
- Uncertainty of company's future
- Hostile work environment
- Person / role mismatch
- Interpersonal relationships (with staff and management)
- Compensation (pay and benefits)

On a related note, studies suggest people leave their bosses not their jobs. Here are the most common reasons. Management –

- Failed to keep promises made to associate
- Failed to give credit to deserving associate
- Ignored the associate, even employing 'the silent treatment'
- Spoke to others about the associate in an openly negative way

In the face of all these factors and determinants there are certain influences in the workplace that cause job satisfaction, as well as a separate set which cause dissatisfaction. Frederick Hertzberg, a psychologist, theorized that job satisfaction and job dissatisfaction act independently of each other. His theory became known as Hertzberg's Motivation-Hygiene Theory.

He posited the following to summarize his theory:

1. Job characteristics that relate to what an individual *does* have the capacity to fulfill his need for achievement, competency, status, personal worth and self-realization. However, the absence of these characteristics does not lead to unhappiness and dissatisfaction. (Motivation factors)
2. Dissatisfaction results from unfavorable assessments of extrinsic factors – company policies, supervision, salary and benefits, interpersonal job relationships, working conditions and job security. However, the presence of these only ensures the associate is not dissatisfied. (Hygiene factors)

If you begin your analysis with an individual who is both dissatisfied and unmotivated, improving Hygiene factors will bring about an individual who is no longer dissatisfied, but remains unmotivated. Then, once you have improved the Motivation factors, you will have an individual who is both satisfied and motivated.

Therefore, if management desires to increase job satisfaction, they should be concerned with the factors raised in the first point. If, however, management wishes to decrease dissatisfaction, they must focus on the areas highlighted in the second point. Paying attention to both sets of factors, Hygiene and Motivation, would stimulate the associate on both fronts.

I provide all this material for you to consider as you reflect on why you resigned, or are considering resigning, job positions. Additionally, I urge you to consider these points as you apply your focus to new and challenging opportunities. Pay attention to both sets of factors.

Herzberg argued that job enrichment is required for intrinsic motivation, and that it is a continuous and ongoing process. Accordingly, he stressed you should reflect on the following:

- The job should have sufficient challenge to utilize my full ability.
- Those of us who demonstrate increasing levels of ability should be afforded increasing levels of responsibility.
- If a job cannot be designed to use my full abilities, then the firm should consider automating the task or replacing me with

someone of a lower level or skill. If I cannot be fully utilized, then there will be a motivational problem.

As you perform your self-discovery and prepare for the next leg of your career, keep these factors in mind. They will serve you well.
To briefly summarize what we've learned so far:

- People don't leave jobs, they leave people
- Job satisfaction results from factors related to job-enrichment
- Dissatisfaction arises from external factors outside our control

Chapter Worksheet
Dead-End Jobs

Why have I left jobs in the past?

What are my job motivators? What must be present for me to love my job?

What is my key takeaway from this chapter?

The Grass Isn't Always Greener

"Life is what you make it. Always has been. Always will be."

~ELEANOR ROOSEVELT

I was having coffee recently with my good friend, Michael, an executive for a large manufacturer. We were discussing job satisfaction and debating the topic of happiness when he stated, "If you had asked me four months ago if I was happy in my job, I would have told you absolutely not. I could think of a dozen reasons why I wasn't happy. Actually, I had received strong interest from a firm in the Southwest and was contemplating relocating my whole family there." Then Michael made a very revealing point about a question that everyone must think about before giving up the job they have. "I asked myself if I was running away from my current job or running toward the new opportunity." He was spot on in his reflection. Too many times people talk themselves into leaving their current job thinking the new position will offer total contentment and bliss. I found this conversation to be so provocative that it demanded further research and evaluation. It led me to consider this one single, central question:

What is happiness?

In a 2004 paper authored by Martin E. P. Seligman, Acacia C. Parks and Tracy Steen titled *a balanced psychology and a full life*, the authors identify three constituents of happiness: pleasure (or positive emotion), engagement and meaning. Later supported by empirical evidence from a 2005 study (Peterson et al 2005), they went on to elaborate: "We call a tendency to pursue happiness by boosting positive emotion, 'the pleasant life'; the tendency to pursue happiness via gratifications, 'the good life'; and the tendency to pursue happiness via using our strengths towards something larger than ourselves, 'the meaningful life'. A person who uses all three routes to happiness leads the 'full life', and those who lead the full life have much the greater life satisfaction." This is a profound perspective.

As I explore these levels of happiness attainment as steps toward bliss, I realized the difficulty and steepness of the climb upward. Leading a pleasant life (pleasure) requires minimal personal investment. We enjoy the good times from the past (what we have to be thankful for, what we've accomplished, relationships dear to us), the good times of the present (being present and in the moment to cherish and honor what we do have and are accomplishing), and our outlook of the future (optimism, anticipation and hope). When we reach out for the good life, it becomes a bit more difficult. Here we must become fully absorbed by something. This could entail completing a difficult assignment, training for certification or teaching a class. Whatever the example, we must draw on our strengths to be successful. But it's all within our capabilities. To achieve a meaningful life, we need to stretch beyond what's comfortable. It gives life purpose and meaning. Think about people who have dedicated their lives to something bigger than themselves, even as they made self-sacrifices that they knew would limit their personal material gain – Mother Teresa, Neil Armstrong, and Martin Luther King come to mind. And how about stay-at-home moms or dads who devote much of their lives to raising children and grandchildren to be productive citizens in our society? In these examples, being present, authentic and expressive in order to help develop character, integrity and a value system in others is such a tremendous gift and requires great personal commitment and sacrifice.

When you can experience the happiness that is realized at all three levels - pleasure, engagement and meaning - you can most rightfully attest to living a full life.

So what do we do with this fresh understanding? For me, it is clear that there are common characteristics to attaining happiness: optimism and positive outlook, frenetic energy to move something forward, self-confidence and determination to be successful - even at the risk of failure, and the idea of learning and growing through full immersion. As you consider these characteristics, you might wish to add or supplant some of your own. That's permitted, as you are best at describing your spectrum of happiness and what "go-to" characteristics you have to achieve your personal bliss.

When you are considering leaving your present job for another, please do answer the question Michael posed to himself, "Am I running away from my current job or running toward the new opportunity?" When you perform an evaluation of your present position within your present company, consider the following job-related factors in your assessment to determine how each measures up on your satisfaction meter:

- Flexibility in work schedule
- Working remotely (and from home)
- Coworkers chemistry and respect
- Adequate benefits package
- Minimal stress level
- Little or no business travel
- Ongoing training
- Opportunity for personal and professional growth
- Community outreach and volunteerism
- Location, location, location
- Reputation (your own and that of your company)
- Quality of life

Also ask yourself –
Do I see a rise in my stress level as Sunday night comes on?
Do I dread going to work on Monday mornings?

Further, determine your true motivators –
Why am I considering leaving my current job?
Have I really worked to improve my current situation?

Your proverbial grass doesn't get lush and green all by itself! You have to tend to it, adding water, fertilizer and much care. This was the conclusion Michael made when he really got down to evaluating what he had in hand. "I know I've not invested what's necessary to improve my current job. I need to do that. I want to do that."

Chapter Worksheet
The Grass Isn't Always Greener

Have I achieved a "meaningful life?" Explain.

What do I believe are MY personal characteristics necessary to attaining happiness and bliss?

What am I "running to"? What attracts me?

Do I look forward to going to work in the morning, and look forward to coming home at night?

What is my key takeaway from this chapter?

You in the Mirror

"Which way do I go from here?"
"That depends on where you want to go."
"I don't know where I am going."
"Then it doesn't matter which way you go."

~ LEWIS CAROLL

There are two common mistakes that many people make when selecting their next career path. One is not spending enough time ensuring their next career is a viable choice. The other is lying to themselves in order to try to convince themselves to follow a career path that is false. When you stand before your reflection in the mirror, take serious note of your imperfections, experiences and laugh lines, and also make an inventory of the assets at your disposal.

Ask yourself if you are like the person I touched on in an earlier chapter, the person who was distorted by adulation and success. If so, the following points bear critical consideration. Regardless, reflect and focus on these key topics:

- Hold yourself accountable. Stop playing the victim. Being out of work is rarely totally someone else's fault or doing. Own up to your transgressions and shortcomings.
- Begin serving others – rather than being served by others. Remember when you first heard, "It is better to give than it is to receive"? Practice this regularly.

- Remember how you got here. What was it that got everyone's attention?
- Be someone's mentor, someone's champion. Look for yourself in others – those key attributes that helped advance your career.
- Check your emotional bandwidth. Don't allow yourself to get too high or too low. I often tell my golfing friends when they have wild swings in their game that you're never as good as your lowest score, but you're also not as bad as your highest score. Keep an even keel.
- Look closely at yourself in the mirror. Remove the mask, veil and any war paint that remains. Find that person that makes you most proud.
- Know this: you are perfect in your imperfections. You are a unique gift to this world. Believe, as the familiar song refrain is written, "You're going to make it after all."

It is critical that you take the time necessary to classify the things that bring you bliss in your work life. Do you enjoy work-life balance? Do you mind giving up weekends for your job on a regular basis? Do you mind an erratic, unpredictable nature to your schedule? Do you wish to work in one-person teams, isolated from other demands and team dynamics? Are you a sit-at-your-desk type of person, or do you enjoy the vitality and energy from working alongside others? These are but some of the dimensions to consider when standing before the mirror, looking at your reflection.

I was working with someone recently who was newly unemployed and was evaluating many possible career choices. She mentioned giving great consideration to some franchise opportunities and other entrepreneur-type investments. As we talked in more detail, I discovered she has two children, one who has special needs, requiring expensive medications and frequent medical services. "Patty, if I had to prioritize the needs in your life right now as they pertain to your next career role, I would be striving for strong family benefits and a flexible working environment." Patty reflected upon this and I added, "Additionally, franchises and options of starting your own business will require major sacrifices and serious investments in your time. Can you really accept these conditions at this time in your life?" It soon became apparent that Patty had not thought through the full ramifications of her plight and was centrally focused on this fresh opportunity. She had not established her priorities, an action necessary to compile the most sensible and honest array of career choices, and to ensure the best use of her time. We'll discuss the concept of applying lenses and filters to derive choices that match up with your priorities (personal, family, life) in a later chapter.

Consider accessing the wisdom and counsel of trusted others as you embark upon this early stage of reentry into the workplace. A spouse or the nucleus of good friends can assist you with your personal assessment. Plead and beg them to be candid and honest in their assessment of you. Urge them to make a list of the things you can improve upon. I can't impress enough the importance of this step as it lays the foundational block for everything else we will discuss going forward. Some of you might wish to carefully consider the spouse evaluation. I was reminded by my good friend, Matt, that it's much like responding to the question your wife might ask, "Honey, do I look fat in this dress?" What I will strongly stress to you is this: go to where you are confident and certain to receive unbridled, honest and constructive feedback. Like it or not, agree with it or not, you need to be made aware of how others perceive you.

Gregg, a good friend who transitioned from Chicago, recently shared this account with me. "I discovered a strong networking group. We called ourselves the 'Thanksgiving Accountability Group' or TAG. Our objective was to assist each other in finding a job by Thanksgiving that year - a mere four months away." Gregg went on to describe his thought process as he looked in the mirror and found himself looking for a new job. "I did feel it was personal. It was happening to me, not to some stranger. While I didn't think it was fair, I did hold myself accountable for my situation. I quickly realized that I needed to move forward – I needed to have a plan. I began by setting weekly goals for myself. How many calls am I going to make? How many networking meetings am I going to go on? What was my story to share with everyone? I received good coaching early on – write the date of the deadline that you are setting for yourself on a sticky note. Place the note on a mirror or in a prominent location to serve as a reminder as well as a motivator. I wrote down 'November 26.' That was my deadline for finding my next job. That became my focus." (See Figure 4).

Figure 4

I asked Gregg what he did if the deadline passed. He replied, "I scratched out that date and set a new one, but I wrote it on the existing note as a reminder." (See Figure 5).

Figure 5

His last piece of advice to me was this: "I do think starting and ending each day giving thanks was critical to maintaining perspective and ultimately to my success." I think Gregg's advice will help many who are struggling with how to begin.

A last note to ponder, consider and place in your heart:

Love the person you see in that mirror. You will spend an eternity with him/her.

Chapter Worksheet
You in the Mirror

What brings me bliss in my work life?

Who are my two or three "go-to" resources that will help me through this transition?

If I honestly reflect on my professional behaviors and operating demeanor, what will I work hard to change or improve upon?

What is my key takeaway from this chapter?

Confidence

"No one can make you feel inferior without your consent"

~ ELEANOR ROOSEVELT

Before you even consider stepping into your first interview, pause and reflect on how you are feeling about yourself, about the job search and about interviewing. If you've just been laid off, or have been "looking" for a while, your self-esteem is likely low or maybe even on empty. Now is the most critical time that you must invest in yourself. You must release the pain of the past. Remember that you've already lived it once, so there is no need to subject yourself to the pain a second time. What's done is done. Bury it. Detach yourself from the event. Conclude that being released was not personal, but, in fact, was a difficult business decision. Tell yourself that this is the best thing that could have happened to you. (Although the timing might be poor, many unemployed people conclude they feel liberated and can now pursue a more suitable future.) Pick yourself up and move forward.

I worked with Gail on a local charity board. Gail is a 30-year regional bank president who was recently released through a corporate restructuring program. While she never saw it coming and could have become withdrawn and paralyzed as she came to grips with being let go, she left without any bitterness or anger. "It was a business decision and I get that," she was quoted saying. She harnessed all her energy to move forward, not wanting to waste time reliving the past. She went on to add, "Everybody is accountable for themselves. I don't want to hear how it's the company's fault."

You must believe in yourself before you can passionately market yourself to another potential employer. When you believe you are the best at what you do, you will lose the feeling of being "pretty good," "adequate," or "above average."

Think back over your career. Where were you at your best? If you could create the ideal role for you, what would it encompass? Are you a fixer who accepts constant change, or do you like to maintain a steady environment of status quo? Do you prefer to operate independently and have responsibility for no one other than yourself, or do you revel in leading others? Do you seek the thrill of big challenges and the spotlight that follows or prefer to be a soldier, responsible for a lesser role, but important nonetheless? Are you detailed-oriented, or are you the 'big picture', conceptual planner? Figure this out and you will be on your way to lighting up your confidence and reengaging in the job market.

How about executive presence? Until you have reclaimed a strong sense of self, you will not be able to elevate your persona to emit this important quality. If you are so worried about yourself, how you are coming across, what to say, what areas to be sure to cover, you will not be at peace and able to reflect a calmness and an aura of confident professionalism - this is the impression you are striving to deliver and to be remembered for.

Dr. Albert Mehrabian, a social scientist who worked at UCLA and MIT, developed a communications model establishing an understanding of body language and non-verbal communications. The value of his theory relates to communications where emotional content is significant. As he studied the effects of the verbal, vocal and visual components of an individual's message, he measured their importance. The verbal aspect, the spoken words actually chosen, only represented 7% of the message's impact. The vocal aspect, paralinguistic (tone, volume, speed, pause), measured 38% of the impact, while the visual component, what the person was doing while the words were being expressed, measured the greatest impact of the message at 55%. Because the visual component of any message is so significant, I would urge you to focus on two things in each interview: be present and be authentic. To deliver with passion and self-assurance, you must strive to be real and in the moment.

In their book, *Leadership Presence*, authors Belle Halpern and Kathy Lubar state, "Great leaders, like great actors, must be confident, energetic, empathetic, inspirational, credible, and authentic." They go further to discuss the need for "Being Present, to be completely in the moment, and flexible enough to handle the unexpected…. to accept yourself, to be authentic, and to reflect your values in your decisions and actions."

As you prepare for each interview think about these attributes. Are you committed to being present and in the moment? Being real and authentic? The interview is not rehearsal. The curtain is up, you are on stage and you must deliver the most compelling and authentic response to their inquiries and stated needs.

> "If you are present, you are alert, fluid, clear, and
> able to welcome all things."

> ~ Lao-Tzu

Chapter Worksheet
Confidence

Am I harboring anger or resentment from losing my most recent job, and if so, do I pledge to release those feelings and focus on my future?

What is my "ideal" job? What job characteristics would get me up each morning looking forward to going to work?

What is my key takeaway from this chapter?

Your Journey Line

"I believe that life is a journey, often difficult
and sometimes incredibly cruel, but we are well
equipped for it if only we tap into our talents and
gifts and allow them to blossom."

~LES BROWN

At this point in your reflection, it's imperative that you erase any false images or sheen that folks have bestowed upon you over your career, or to this point in your young life, if you are just beginning your career. You know *you* more precisely and completely than anyone else ever will. After all, you've lived with *you* all your life, and you are your own worst critic. You've witnessed your failings even when absent an audience.

When you stop to consider your life to date as a kaleidoscope containing the myriad of your total experiences, both good and not so good, you become quickly humbled. Back in 2005 my company placed an exercise before the entire executive committee. The sixteen of us were instructed to tear a blank sheet of paper from a flip-chart pad and tape it along the wall of our meeting room, making sure there was ample space to work alone, away from the distraction of others. Next, we were asked to take an available marker and draw a horizontal line mid-way down the page, marking from left to right (see Figure 6).

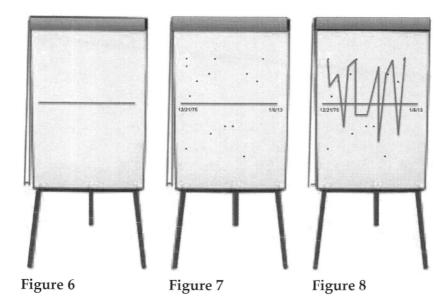

Figure 6   **Figure 7**   **Figure 8**

At the left-most point of our line, we were told to write down the date of our birth, and on the right-most point write down the current date. Once complete, we were directed to reflect back over our lives - both the ups and the downs, the good times and the most difficult times. Going back in time as far as we could remember, we placed a dot with our marker on the page around the time of the event. If the experience was a positive one, the dot was placed above the line. If the experience was a difficult one, the dot went below the line. How high or low you placed your dot above or below the line correlated to how high or how low the event impacted you (see Figure 7).

Finally, we connected our dots across the page (see Figure 8).

While this part of the exercise was difficult, the next part was truly frightening. Each of us had to randomly stand and walk the entire team through our life journey. If done with complete honesty and with an admission of our failures, this placed each of us in a very vulnerable position. Most of us had not shared many, if any, of our points below the line with anyone at work. But that is the true power of this exercise. You had to be comfortable sharing your true self with others. I have to admit that there were three of us (me included) who could not get through our story without a great deal of emotion. This proved to be a very draining evening, physically and emotionally.

Over the course of the next several months, this exercise was carried down through the ranks, inside our departments and into key critical project teams. It proved to be a very successful team-building tool.

You might be asking what types of life events were placed on these journey lines, both above and below the line. As you might expect, everyone found it much easier to highlight those things above the line, their proudest defining moments and accomplishments. Those items included graduating college, getting married, securing that first professional job, having children, changing careers, etc.

Events below the line get darker and more challenging. You're questioning how willing you are to expose yourself and to allow yourself to become most vulnerable. You might be asking yourself what's to be gained by telling it all.

I heard folks describe their journey growing up with physical abuse, racial prejudice, dropping out of college, bankruptcies, divorce, alcoholic parents, mental illness, suicide, job terminations, loss of loved ones, serious illnesses, etc. Heavy and painful experiences, to be sure.

I share this story with you to encourage you to complete this same exercise and imagine telling this story to people who might very well judge you on its content. Be real and be reflective. I have saved a copy of mine and have updated it over the years since. Consider doing the same with yours.

This exercise has a way of stripping away your veils of bravado and perceived power and helping you understand the real *you*. Time has the tendency to place distance and amnesia to our remembrance of painful, earlier experiences. We may be purposefully trying to forget and trudge onward, but it's important that we not forget where we came from and know that it formed who we are today.

Having reestablished your sense of self and regained your elusive air of confidence, you are ready to look at some books that might add immeasurable benefit to your psyche and overall wellbeing.

Chapter Worksheet
Your Journey Line

Was I completely honest in assessing my Journey Line? Did I omit anything?

What areas below the line were most difficult for me to acknowledge?

What is my key takeaway from this chapter?

Recommended Reading

"If one reads enough books one has a fighting chance. Or better, one's chances of survival increase with each book one reads."

~ SHERMAN ALEXIE

Over the course of my career I have become a voracious reader. I consume business material from multiple sources at a rapid pace. It is not unusual for me to have several books open at once, completing on average one per week. The e-reader was a true innovation and gift. It allows me to travel with my whole collection in the space the size of one paperback book. If a friend, colleague or the media recommends a business book, I research it and invariably I purchase it. Sometimes I even purchase both the hardcopy and the digital versions of the same book in order to loan the books to friends more easily.

Ordering dozens of good business books and giving them to clients and colleagues is a great way to share the value in learning and growth.

As I have networked with folks over the years, books have become a shared language, a mutual topic of interest and conversation. I would like to share with you an abbreviated list of books that I have read, shared and recommended to others, and they to me. As many of these are very popular, you might already count them among your own favorites or have them in your collection.

1. **Now, Discover Your Strengths,** by Marcus Buckingham and Donald O. Clifton (Jan. 29, 2001)
"Marcus Buckingham, coauthor of the national bestseller *First, Break All the Rules,* and Donald O. Clifton, Chair of the Gallup International Research & Education Center, have created a revolutionary program to help readers identify their talents, build them into strengths, and enjoy consistent, near-perfect performance. At the heart of the book is the Internet-based StrengthsFinder® Profile, the product of a 25-year, multimillion-dollar effort to identify the most prevalent human strengths. The program introduces 34 dominant "themes" with thousands of possible combinations, and reveals how they can best be translated into personal and career success. In developing this program, Gallup has conducted psychological profiles with more than two million individuals to help readers learn how to focus and perfect these themes." Amazon.com.

2. **Blue Ocean Strategy: How to Create Uncontested Market Space and Make Competition Irrelevant,** by W. Chan Kim and Renee Mauborgne (Feb. 3, 2005)
"Written by the business world's new gurus, *Blue Ocean Strategy* continues to challenge everything you thought you knew about competing in today's crowded market place. Based on a study of 150 strategic moves spanning more than a hundred years and thirty industries, authors W. Chan Kim and Renee Mauborgne argue that lasting success comes from creating 'blue oceans': untapped new market spaces ripe from growth. And the business world has caught on - companies around the world are skipping the bloody red oceans of rivals and creating their very own blue oceans. With over one million copies sold world wide, *Blue Ocean Strategy* is quickly reaching "must read" status among smart business readers. Have you caught the wave?" Amazon.com.

3. **Start With Why: How Great Leaders Inspire Everyone to Take Action**, by Simon Sinek (Dec. 27, 2011)
Starting with Why works in big business and small business, in the nonprofit world and in politics. Those who start with Why never manipulate, they inspire. And people follow them not because they have to; they follow because they want to.

Drawing on a wide range of real-life stories, Sinek weaves together a clear vision of what it truly takes to lead and inspire. This book is for anyone who wants to inspire others or who wants to find someone to inspire them.

4. **How Will You Measure Your Life?** By Clayton M. Christensen, James Allworth and Karen Dillon (May 15, 2012)

"In 2010 world-renowned innovation expert Clayton M. Christensen gave a powerful speech to the Harvard Business School's graduating class. Drawing upon his business research, he offered a series of guidelines for finding meaning and happiness in life. He used examples from his own experiences to explain how high achievers can all too often fall into traps that lead to unhappiness.

The speech was memorable not only because it was deeply revealing but also because it came at a time of intense personal reflection: Christensen had just overcome the same type of cancer that had taken his father's life. As Christensen struggled with the disease, the question "How do you measure your life?" became more urgent and poignant, and he began to share his insights more widely with family, friends, and students.

In this groundbreaking book, Christensen puts forth a series of questions: How can I be sure that I'll find satisfaction in my career? How can I be sure that my personal relationships become enduring sources of happiness? How can I avoid compromising my integrity — and stay out of jail? Using lessons from some of the world's greatest businesses, he provides incredible insights into these challenging questions.

How Will You Measure Your Life? is full of inspiration and wisdom, and will help students, midcareer professionals, and parents alike forge their own paths to fulfillment." Amazon.com.

5. **Chapters: Create a Life of Exhilaration and Accomplishment in the Face of Change,** by Candice Carpenter (Dec. 30, 2002)

"Her own genuinely encouraging chapters take the reader through the various stages of closing an old chapter and opening a new one. . . . She offers genuine help by giving people the words to understand and describe what they are going through as they close and open chapters of their lives." Publishers Weekly

"In Chapters, author Candice Carpenter offers concrete, step-by-step guidance for planning ahead for major changes, knowing when it's time to shift gears and embark on a new chapter, handling false starts and failures, and achieving true personal satisfaction over a lifetime." Amazon.com.

6. **Never Eat Alone: And Other Secrets to Success, One Relationship at a Time**, by Keith Ferrazzi and Tahl Raz (Feb. 22, 2005)

"Do you want to get ahead in life? Climb the ladder to personal success? '

The secret, master networker Keith Ferrazzi claims, is in reaching out to other people. As Ferrazzi discovered early in life, what distinguishes highly successful people from everyone else is the way they use the power of relationships — so that everyone wins.

In *Never Eat Alone*, Ferrazzi lays out the specific steps — and inner mindset — he uses to reach out to connect with the thousands of colleagues, friends, and associates on his Rolodex, people he has helped and who have helped him. This provides great guidance.

The son of a small-town steelworker and a cleaning lady, Ferrazzi first used his remarkable ability to connect with others to pave the way to a scholarship at Yale, a Harvard MBA, and several top executive posts. Not yet out of his thirties, he developed a network of relationships that stretched from Washington's corridors of power to Hollywood's A-list, leading to him being named one of Crain's 40 Under 40 and selected as a Global Leader for Tomorrow by the Davos World Economic Forum.

Ferrazzi's form of connecting to the world around him is based on generosity, helping friends connect with other friends. Ferrazzi distinguishes genuine relationship building from the crude, desperate glad-handling usually associated with "networking." He then distills his system of reaching out to people into practical, proven principles:

Don't keep score: It's never simply about getting what you want. It's about getting what you want and making sure that the people who are important to you get what they want, too.

"Ping" constantly: The Ins and Outs of reaching out to those in your circle of contacts all the time—not just when you need something.

Never eat alone: The dynamics of status are the same whether you're working at a corporation or attending a society event— "invisibility" is a fate worse than failure. Make yourself more visible.

In the course of the book, Ferrazzi outlines the timeless strategies shared by the world's most connected individuals, from Katherine Graham to Bill Clinton, Vernon Jordan to the Dalai Lama.

Chock full of specific advice on handling rejection, getting past gatekeepers, becoming a "conference commando," and more, *Never Eat Alone* is destined to take its place alongside *How to Win Friends and Influence People* as an inspirational classic." Amazon.com.

7. **Excuse Me, Your Life Is Waiting: The Astonishing Power of Feelings**, by Lynn Grabhorn (Mar. 1, 2003)

"Upbeat, humorous, and iconoclastic, Lynn Grabhorn introduced readers to the Law of Attraction in 2000 with *Excuse Me, Your Life Is Waiting*. The hardcover edition was an immediate hit, sold more than 151,000 copies, and appeared on the *New York Times* bestseller list.

Grabhorn was the first to reveal that the power of feelings is what unconsciously shapes and molds every moment of every day. In this ground-breaking book, she reveals how paying attention to feelings—rather than positive thinking, or sweat and strain, or good or bad luck, or even smarts—is the way to change your life, make dreams come true, and create the kind of life you really want to live. *Excuse Me, Your Life Is Waiting* is filled with logical explanations, simple steps, and true-life examples that empower readers to access their feelings and turn their lives around." Amazon.com.

8. **What's Your Story? Storytelling to Move Markets, Audiences, People, and Brands**, by Ryan Mathews and Watts Wacker (Aug. 30, 2007)

"Storytelling is the universal human activity. Every society, at every stage of history, has told stories–and listened to them intently, passionately. Stories are how people tell each other who they are, where they came from, how they're unique, what they believe. Stories capture their memories of the past and their hopes for the future. Stories are one more thing, too: They are your most powerful, most underutilized tool for competitive advantage. Whether you know it or not, your business is already telling stories. What's Your Story? will help you take control of those stories and make them work for you. Legendary business thinkers Ryan Mathews and Watts Wacker reveal how to craft an unforgettable story...create the back story that makes it believable...make sure your story cuts through today's relentless bombardment of consumer messages...and gets heard, remembered, and acted on." Amazon.com.

9. **Leadership Presence**, by Belle Linda Halpern and Kathy Lubar (Oct. 14, 2004)

"For more than a decade, Belle Linda Halpern and Kathy Lubar have applied the lessons and expertise they have learned as performing artists to the work of their company, The Ariel Group. Halpern and Lubar have helped tens of thousands of executives at major companies around the country and the globe, including General Electric, Mobil Oil, Capital One, and Deloitte. In *Leadership Presence*, they make their time-tested strategies available to everyone, from high-profile CEOs to young professionals seeking promotion. Their practical, proven approach will enable you to develop the skills necessary to inspire confidence, command respect, build credibility, and motivate others. Halpern and Lubar teach you:
* How to handle tough situations with heightened confidence and flexibility
* How to build your relationships to enhance collaboration and business development
* How to express yourself dramatically and motivate others
* How to integrate your personal values into communication to inspire others and become a more effective leader" Amazon.com

10. **Give and Take: A Revolutionary Approach to Success**, by Adam M. Grant Ph.D. (Apr. 9, 2013)

"For generations, we have focused on the individual drivers of success: passion, hard work, talent, and luck. But today, success is increasingly dependent on how we interact with others. It turns out that at work, most people operate as takers, matchers, or givers. Whereas takers strive to get as much as possible from others and matchers aim to trade evenly, givers are the rare breed of people who contribute to others without expecting anything in return.

Using his own pioneering research as Wharton's youngest tenured professor, Grant shows that these styles have a surprising impact on success. Although some givers get exploited and burn out, the rest achieve extraordinary results across a wide range of industries. Combining cutting-edge evidence with captivating stories, this landmark book shows how one of America's best networkers developed his connections, why the creative genius behind one of the most popular shows in television history toiled for years in anonymity, how a basketball executive responsible for multiple draft busts transformed his franchise into a winner, and how we could have anticipated Enron's demise four years before the company collapsed-without ever looking at a single number." Amazon.com

11. **The Power of Myth**, by Joseph Campbell and Bill Moyers (collaborator) (Jun. 1, 1991)

    This is a book you will want to keep close to you forever. It traverses many topics and areas of interest. A few of the chapter titles that I often refer to: The Journey Inward, The First Storytellers, Sacrifice and Bliss and Masks of Eternity. Joseph Campbell drives home the point that, "When you're on a journey, and the end keeps getting further and further away, then you realize that the real end is the journey."

12. **Man's Search For Meaning**, by Victor E. Frankl (Jun. 1, 2006)

    "Psychiatrist Viktor Frankl's memoir has riveted generations of readers with its descriptions of life in Nazi death camps and its lessons for spiritual survival. Between 1942 and 1945 Frankl labored in four different camps, including Auschwitz, while his parents, brother, and pregnant wife perished. Based on his own experience and the experiences of those he treated in his practice, Frankl argues that we cannot avoid suffering but we can choose how to cope with it, find meaning in it, and move forward with renewed purpose. Frankl's theory—known as logotherapy, from the Greek word logos ("meaning")—holds that our primary drive in life is not pleasure, as Freud maintained, but the discovery and pursuit of what we personally find meaningful.

At the time of Frankl's death in 1997, Man's Search for Meaning had sold more than 10 million copies in twenty-four languages. A 1991 reader survey by the Library of Congress and the Book-of-the-Month Club that asked readers to name a "book that made a difference in your life" found Man's Search for Meaning among the ten most influential books in America." Beacon Press.

Chapter Worksheet
Recommended Reading

What books from this list am I going to commit to reading?

What books have I read that I would want to add to my Recommended Reading list and suggest to others?

What is my takeaway from this chapter?

Section Worksheet
Reflection

What are my top 3 takeaways from this section, Reflection?

-
-
-

That's right, STOP!

Before you proceed to the next section, Preparation, you need to carefully consider the foundation this section, Reflections, has formed beneath you.

> Do you still have doubts and unanswered questions?
> Has Reflections improved your outlook at all?
> Do you fully know the real *you*?

Do not rush the process. If you have any lingering doubt or feelings about really knowing yourself, I urge you to return to the beginning of this section and re-read all its chapters. The section should have been a struggle.

Ask yourself...

> Do I hold myself accountable for all of my actions and for who I am?
> Have I validated my self-assessment through others?
> Can I define what's missing from living a "full life"?
> Can I master doing nothing without guilt?
> Have I gained insight into my positive transformation and my attitude of gratitude?
> Did I find my quiet place for reflection? How many hours did I invest there to better understand myself?

If you have **<u>any</u>** question about the validity and honesty of your answers here, you shouldn't go on. You should return to the beginning of this section and get gritty. I wasn't kidding when I said this section would be your most labor-intensive. You must put in the requisite time.

There are no shortcuts to excellence...

Okay, enough. Decision time. Go back, or go on.

Interlude

"There is no exercise better for the heart than
reaching down and lifting people up."

~ JOHN HOLMES

I take this pause in our Reflection journey to introduce you to the idea of enlightenment through giving. In 2005, I was very fortunate to be introduced to Noel Tichy. As part of my previous company's transformational leadership training, we engaged Noel to instruct us and raise our awareness of "the teaching organization," "the transformational leader" and "the cycle of leadership."

Noel is a gifted American management consultant, author and educator. He has co-authored, edited, or contributed to over 30 books and was the director of global development at GE's Crotonville. Over the course of our time together, he reiterated his passion for joining leadership excellence to a model of serving others. He is staunch in his position of returning back to the community the leadership lessons we had acquired and practiced. He knows the community is strengthened and nourished by this continual consumption of knowledge. He impressed me with his emphasis on, and passion for, caring.

As you wrap up your time in Reflection, I want to put a fine point on getting real, getting gritty and getting re-acquainted with yourself. Please indulge me by visiting the website below and learning more about one man, Scott Harrison, Founder & CEO of Charity:Water. After losing his way early in his life, this man came to discover himself after deep reflection and introspection. An entire decade of his life (18-28) was consumed with self-absorption and a stout 'not enough' persona. He transformed himself and climbed the heights of his discovery to lead a cause that helped 800 million individuals – a feat almost beyond comprehension. It proves to me that everything is possible if you have the vision, the conviction and the relentless passion to see it through.

http://www.youtube.com/watch?v=XLdDMDkwK1s

If you watched the entire 47:39 minutes of the presentation, I feel certain it affected you in a number of ways. Principally, I hope you realized that people can, and often do, return to a place that is more rewarding and redeeming than where they might be at the present time. You simply have to want it bad enough. It wasn't until Scott declared, "I was the most spiritually, emotionally, [and] morally bankrupt person that I knew and I needed to make a change." He described being in a very "dark" part of his life. Making change and seeking true happiness doesn't occur overnight - it requires a lot of time and effort. But it's worth it!

2.Preparation

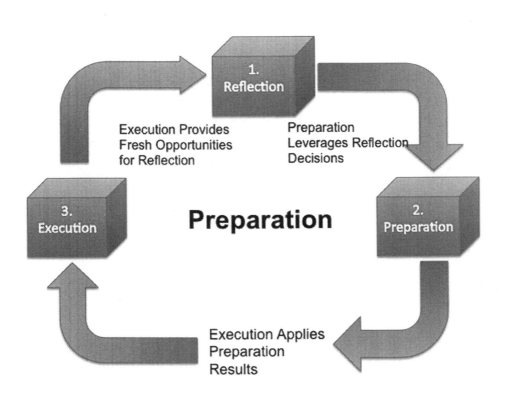

Networking

"A year from now you will wish you had started today."

~ KAREN LAMB

Some of the people I have met with have developed and honed a networking muscle that will serve them well throughout their career journey. How much time have you spent getting out, becoming more visible, meeting new people, forging new relationships, while deepening others? Are you comfortable speaking in front of groups? Have you joined civic or charity committees? Are you comfortable serving on community or neighborhood boards? Where do your passions lie? Academics and education? Sports and coaching? Mentoring? Financial planning? Youth at risk? Aging and older adults? Services that care for the downtrodden, the homeless? Are you a member of a book club, social or dinner club or athletic club?

"He who knows others is wise. He who knows himself is enlightened"

~ LAO TZU

Networking is not a once and done activity. It is not a means to an end, but an endless journey. In these most difficult employment markets, what will distinguish you and supply a decisive edge is the powerful use of your network. The more people you know and can call on for counsel and assistance will provide tremendous traction as you search for that ideal job role.

Matt Younquist, president of Career Horizons, observed, "At least 70 percent, if not 80 percent of the jobs are not published. And yet most people – they are spending 70 or 80 percent of their time surfing the net versus getting out there talking to employers, taking some chances [and] realizing that the vast majority of hiring is friends and acquaintances hiring other trusted friends and acquaintances."

Randall Powell, author of *Career Planning Strategies: Hire Me!*, "The web and other publications list only about 20 percent of available jobs."

A 2012 study conducted by Right Management of more than 46,000 out-of-work individuals revealed that networking was 46 percent effective at helping job seekers find new employment.

When you consider the art of networking, you might be intimidated for varying reasons. As with interviewing, much time might have elapsed since you built or expanded your network. Take the necessary time to go through your own introspection. Find your passions, those things you can easily converse on. Sitting across the table from Spencer, a graduating college senior, I read his nervousness and tried to find topics to break the ice. Once I uncovered his passions, the ice melted and vanished. Ninety minutes passed in a hurry and we were able to touch on many things that helped him on his journey of self-discovery.

If you are shy and introverted, apply your listening skills. Find topics that will allow you to highlight more about you and your strengths, and what you have to offer potential employers. Start your networking on safe ground by meeting with those you know well and who know you. This will allow you to get into a rhythm and to develop your shtick, your spiel, your story. An important element for you to master is your presence. Before each networking meeting invest time to best understand your contact. Remove all distractions from your mind. Be completely invested - physically, mentally and emotionally - to each networking meeting. Stay focused.

When you set out to meet with anyone, have a plan in hand. Make it a point that you are going to learn something from every networking interaction. While every meeting is sure to uncover or introduce new material, at a minimum prepare a game plan for what you wish to discuss. Don't waste someone's time by expecting him or her to carry the entire discussion. You need to lead with confidence and have topics with you germane to each networking discussion. Begin keeping a journal to collect your take-aways. You will treasure this collection from your journey. Keep in mind – Relationships Matter. Invest fully of yourself.

In ensuing chapters, you will learn the mechanics of constructing your personal marketing plan. First, we will begin with establishing your priorities (lenses & filters) to apply to your job search. From there we will research and identify the companies whose profiles flow nicely through your filters. Then we will discuss prioritizing those selected companies into your personal Top 10, ranking them and segmenting them (perhaps primary, secondary and tertiary). From there we will explore building a contact list of people you know within those companies you have an interest in interviewing with. For those primary companies, it is imperative that you expend considerable effort to identify multiple contacts - those with influence and those who possess reference-ability. If you've been building upon an established network over your career, this effort will not prove daunting at all. But, as the latest collapse in our economy and job market revealed, many long-term associates were being let go who had not spent meaningful (if any) time establishing their network.

After I successfully worked with a candidate through his job search over a number of months, he called me up and asked me to meet with him over morning coffee. "What a relief! I made it." Tom happily stated. "Thanks for your help. It was nice to have someone by my side as I made this journey." He pointed to his thick manila folder encompassing all his networking activities as he said, "Now I can finally get rid of this thing!" I was shocked. "This *thing,* as you call it, is the biggest reason you found your new job. Do not discard that collection. You put all that effort into networking and you need to keep it alive. Add to it. Keep it current and up to date. Make it a priority to expand your network. You have worked too hard for too long to simply cast it aside," I responded. People who don't see the value in networking, but see it as a task, a single event, a beginning to an end, will likely need to recreate the effort down the road when they find themselves looking for that next job. Equally as important, they will not have this resource to help introduce others into a company with which they have good familiarity. They will lose the opportunity to optimally help others.

Adam Grant, author of the best-selling book, *Give and Take*, separates individuals into three categories: givers, matchers and takers. Givers contribute to others, expecting nothing in return. They make the time available to help and encourage others. The satisfaction that givers receive is in the value gained by others. I feel this powerful sensation often when individuals leave a meeting with me with renewed energy, passion and confidence. Takers, those who strive to get as much as possible from others, can exploit givers. They seek to win in every exchange. They tend to use people for their own gain. Matchers, on the other hand, give when they can see an equivalent gain being returned. They will meet with someone who they think will benefit them in the future. We all possess the muscle to be givers – some of us have built up that muscle through continued use. Carefully consider these classifications: giver, matcher and taker. Which category describes you?

An important part of networking is preparing and presenting a public face for others to become acquainted with. I've networked with individuals who have created their own personal website that lets people know more about their capabilities and accomplishments. If they have written papers or authored professional blogs, these are made available through the website. But be careful to draw a distinction between your personal and professional lives. When the two are blended, the viewer loses emphasis in his primary interest by being presented a secondary, less essential aspect of who you are. It can be confusing to see your professional background interspersed with vacation pictures and family activities. LinkedIn provides a repository for professionals to outline their interests, background, and job history, and at the same time create connections with others in your expanding network. Essentially, the more people can learn about you, the more opportunities your network will attract and, as it expands, the more likely job opportunities will be presented.

A quick side story about the potential of LinkedIn: As you are developing your personal marketing plan you will undoubtedly be searching for connections to your list of ideal company prospects. Using a professional resource like LinkedIn will greatly aid that particular aspect of your plan. I recently met with a strong recruiter and all-around good guy, Gaelen. As we discussed corporate values and how we each strived to connect others to that next job opportunity, I stressed my willingness to accept connections with as many people as possible who wished to employ LinkedIn to expand their network. I relayed to Gaelen, "I am always disappointed when I discover my LinkedIn connections have hidden or denied access to their contacts. In my view, contacts should be available for all to see. In this difficult economy the more access we all have to the talent around us, the better our chances are of helping others. I have many competitors who have connected with me through LinkedIn and I am committed to having my contacts being completely open to them. What are they trying to protect when they deny access to their contacts?" I noticed a far-away look on Gaelen's face. When I asked him what was troubling him, he responded, "When I get to the office I'm going to ensure I have opened up access to my contacts." He, too, saw the value in that logic.

A good place to start building your network is with friends and previous associates - those who know you, your strengths, your assets and your values.

Through LinkedIn, don't be afraid to ask your network to endorse your skills, and/or compose a recommendation.

Networking is a true 24x7 job everywhere you travel. Social functions, religious settings, sports events and activities – all provide you with opportunities to network and introduce yourself, and to tell your story. As my dear friend, Sydney, relayed to me, "the networking meeting is a moment of giving and receiving for all parties – the most rewarding are when lines of communication are blurred and roles are reversed through dialogue." Amen, Syd!

Construct a more formal contact database. Keep track of people you know, people you meet, and where they work along with other companies to which they might be willing to introduce you. Make sure you include adequate contact information - cell phone number and e-mail addresses. Also, consider a sort of personal rating system for how influential each resource might be to your search. This will save you time down the road as your number of contacts grows.

It really is about who you know that will launch you to your next professional opportunity. It starts and ends with networking. Don't minimize the impact of tilling and fertilizing that garden, for the harvest you reap will provide bountiful production in the way of personal and professional growth and awareness.

"Every exit is an entry somewhere else."

~TOM STOPPARD

Chapter Worksheet
Networking

On a scale of one ("scared and intimidated") to five ("natural and professional"), where do I rank myself as a networker?

What steps am I going to take to improve my networking?

Am I a giver, taker or matcher? What is my philosophy on giving?

What is my takeaway from this chapter?

Practice, Practice, Practice

"It's a little like wrestling a gorilla. You don't quit when you're tired."

~ ROBERT STRAUSS

Most of us are not professional interviewers. We invest our immediate future with our employer and give it our total devotion. When the time is upon us to find that next job challenge, many things are at play and the far majority of them are negative. The list of emotions includes fear, uncertainty, doubt, anger, anxiety and unease. Our self-confidence has been shattered. We become desperate. We are out of practice.

I routinely encourage people to practice interviewing on a regular basis. This entails keeping your resume updated, knowing your story (who you are, what you've done, where you would like to go) and developing an individual presence. (These areas will be discussed in later chapters.) For now, let's talk about practice. Please consider the following:

- Interviewing for a new job does not require you to accept any offer made to you. That's a fact.
- The more you tell your story, the more you improve. The more you refine it, the more you buy into it. You make it real and you own it.

- If you aren't willing to step out and interview for opportunities that seem unlikely, you will not catch the possibility of the right job presented at the right time, for the right person (YOU!)

I remember a time I was contacted by Jennifer, a local corporate recruiter, requesting a meeting over a cup of coffee to discuss a key opening. I dismissed it without much thought. A few weeks later the ever-determined recruiter called once more. "Please, don't hang up. Won't you have a cup of coffee with me? Lets discuss your market value." At this intersection in life, I distinctly recall thinking to myself, "You have given this advice over most of your career. It's time to follow it; get some practice." Later that week I arrived at 7:00 a.m. for that simple coffee and conversation. I walked out to the parking lot at 6:00 p.m. that night feeling battle-tested and tired, but invigorated. I remember smiling as I thought: "I got practice, all right. I was aptitude tested, drug tested, panel interviewed and quizzed by more individuals than I could recall." Could I have performed better? Yes, without a doubt. Did I make mistakes? Sure, but isn't that what practice is for?

Having given this advice countless times over the years, I remember catching up with an acquaintance who relayed his story. "I told you I wouldn't relocate out of this region, but you convinced me to perfect my story, and increase my self-confidence by expanding my interview reach. I remember you saying, 'that perfect bus may come along when you're not standing at the stop, and it will continue on without you'. I flew out to Kansas to interview for a critical executive position. It felt good. Knowing I wasn't completely sold on the role made it easier to relax. I was more natural, more myself. Guess what? They offered me the job, and even flew my family out to consider neighborhoods and schools. My family voted to turn it down, but it was quite the high to be wanted again!"

You can't turn down any offer you don't receive, because you aren't willing to look.

I was discussing this chapter with Angie, a good friend and successful executive from Atlanta. She posed this question: "Do you recommend practice in moderation? It would seem to be distractive and potentially harmful to relationships if overdone." I think, like any skill, you have to use it to stay sharp. Some people are exceptional interviewers and master communicators. They require less practice relative to the person who lacks confidence or hasn't interviewed in some time. You also need to fit it within your priorities and schedule. This will serve to manage the distractive nature that practicing can introduce. On average, once or twice each year ought to keep you tuned and in condition to perform should you be required to. Pay close attention to all feedback you receive. You should aim to improve with each interview session. Incorporate feedback into your next practice session.

On a related note, I was having coffee one recent morning with Pat, a C-level executive with his firm. Are you familiar with the phrase, "I'm listening, but I just can't hear you"? Well, I had coached Pat for the better part of a year to seek interviewing practice even in good times and even with firms he had little or no interest in working for. Pat smiled as he spoke, "So I went in for an interview to get practice and eventually was not selected for the position. I was ok with that. I did gain interviewing experience that would benefit me down the road. However, many months later I interviewed again for a senior role with that same company. The recruiter floored me when he told me, 'I'm surprised you are back. We didn't think you had any interest in us based on your previous interview.'" Pat had not meant to send that message, and was not aware he had done so. He finished by saying, "now I better understand why you stressed for me to get out and practice."

In summary, no one can force you to accept a position you don't want, but it's nice to be courted, to have a chance to hone your interviewing skills and perfect your story. You only get better with practice and repetition.

"You'll miss the best things if you keep your eyes shut"

~ Dr. Seuss

Chapter Worksheet
Practice, Practice, Practice

On a scale of one ("I don't know where to start") to five ("comfortable and confident"), how do I rate myself as an interviewee, and why?

What am I going to do to improve my comfort and confidence in interviewing?

What is my takeaway from this chapter?

Lenses and Filters

"If you don't know where you are going, you'll end
up some place else."

~ YOGI BERRA

As you embark upon a new job search, it's important to know the factors
of a new job that are attractive to you. In your preplanning consider the
lenses you will use to filter and identify the best employers - those that
best match your needs and desires. I'm sure you will add others, but
here are a few of the most common qualifiers:

- Geography – if you're ever going to expand your search map,
  do it early, at the beginning. The ideal job may come along
  and you haven't yet expanded your reach. Don't allow that to
  happen.
- Industry – some people are born retailers, others prefer financial services or manufacturing. If industry is important, use the
  lens to assure proper clarity and analysis.
- Government or private sector – some people are drawn to support local or state government. You may be leaving long-term
  employment in a state agency. Know yourself well enough to
  decide to either stay the course or start afresh in an entirely new
  area.

- Company size – some people wish to be a "big fish in a small pond." They wish to maximize their impact and be as visible as possible. Others feel larger firms provide greater stability, job security, a smarter workforce; a quality benefits program, etc.
- Noble cause – some are committed to a cause, such as curing cancer, stopping homelessness, etc.
- Eliminating factors – if you will not work in certain environments, e.g., tobacco, alcohol, entertainment industry, foreign manufacturing, etc., it is best to know that up front.

It's imperative that you establish the filters that are most meaningful to you. The idea is to identify the most desirable firms in which you would consider making an investment. (The investment is YOU!) This is the first step in preparing your personal marketing plan. If you don't get this step right, you are misaligned right out of the gate. Other filters people apply include growth versus stability, climate and weather, schools, diversity, major cities and airports, nearby water and/or mountains, taxes and political position, parks and recreation, and/or professional sports, among a myriad of others.

Mike, a very good friend and successful executive, extended some of his own experience when he recruited and interviewed prospective employees. "I would ask them to rank order the importance of the company you work for – for some it's important to work for a big, brand name company; what you do day to day – job tasks and responsibilities; where you live – do you need a warm climate, big city, proximity to family; the people you work with – culture, age/diversity of employee base; and financial rewards. This framework was used in the past at Westinghouse. I found it to be a good tool."

Additionally, there are many lists that outline the best and worst jobs, the most and least stressful jobs, the most satisfying careers, the fastest growing sectors and the most physically demanding jobs. One particular website, www.careercast.com, provides an array of factors for you to consider when evaluating possible careers.

Remember, it's about finding the absolute best fit for you. If you put forth the effort and energy up front, you will likely find it more enjoying and rewarding at the finish. Know that it will require some deep and honest self-analysis. Where have you been happiest? Where have you been most successful? To the contrary, what environments did you come to hate? What situations did you find cumbersome and loathsome?

Recall the chapter, Personal Values. As you determine the companies that best align with your values, investigate how they treat associates, suppliers and their community. Is there a cheering sound emanating from these circles of constituents? Do they invest in their people? What are they known for? If they express corporate values on their website, have those values been achieved, and do they align well with your own values?

Remember that success hides a lot of sins. When times are good and bountiful, firms are more likely to be more giving and neighborly. It's when times are tough that a firm's values are put to the test. Look for long-term trends. Gain intelligence through the Internet, but with a critical eye. If practical, visit their location. Talk to present and past employees and those who would best know how a company lives up to their values. Be sure their actions are in line with your expectations. You don't wish to be surprised later when it's too late.

On a related note, Larry, a long-time friend and senior manager with one of the world's leading manufacturers, commented on intercultural differences as a key lens or filter. "When I interview prospective candidates for hire, I make it a central point to gain their impressions and insights on what they *think* they know about working for a foreign-led organization," he commented. "There is much to be learned and understood about working in a foreign-dominated company. Do they fully comprehend the cultural differences? The company's way of thinking and reacting to situations is very different than that of U.S. companies. The surroundings and settings are going to be different, some very subtle. Finally, their concept of respect is a big contrast from what you see in the U.S.," he went on to add.

What Larry was pointing out is the need for a full immersion within this section to fully comprehend the company choices best suited to your needs, desires and values. If you are exploring international business opportunities for the first time, you must research and understand more deeply and more broadly the many distinct differences that exist within those firms.

As you outline your thoughts regarding aspects that will be pertinent and germane to your search, let's take a moment to consider a few alternative career paths: Consulting, Entrepreneurship and Working in Nonprofit.

Chapter Worksheet
Lenses and Filters

What factors are critical to me as I consider my next job opportunity?

What are some companies that both attract me and fit my personal lenses and filters?

What is my takeaway from this chapter?

Consulting

"Great ideas need landing gears as well as wings."

~ C. O. JACKSON

When you are contemplating what's next in your career, it's often a good time to reflect on other possible avenues for employment. Should I look into consulting? Should I buy into a franchise? Should I take my skills and talents to the non-profit community of organizations? These questions are a natural extension to the Lenses and Filters chapter.

These areas have risen in prominence during the most recent difficult years. More people began considering these dramatic extensions when they felt they had exhausted areas within their comfort zone.

I recall overhearing a conversation between two external consultants at a time when their project implementation was winding down and they were about to move on. "I'm really going to miss not witnessing the organization realize the many years of benefits from our efforts", Grace stated. "Get over it," her counterpart, Kimberly, responded. "Our job is done and it's time to move on to our next engagement." This exchange struck me as one determinant when considering a consulting career. Do you need to see a project completely through its natural life cycle? Can you be satisfied with your success within a narrower, more limited engagement? If you can't walk away and leave behind the results from your labor and not worry about the future of that work, you might want to reconsider if consulting is the right fit for you.

How do you feel at the end of each workday as you head to the parking lot to your car? Do you carry your work-related troubles home with you? Can you comfortably leave them behind, disengage, and move on to other things? Company employees often discuss the sense of "never being done" when it comes to their work. They take work home on weekends and holidays. They will lie awake planning their next day or next week, mentally managing their inbox. Consultants will tell you that when their day is done, they are done. They can quickly disengage and begin focusing on other things that matter to them. Their days have a distinct beginning and a distinct ending. When they are working for a client, they are always ON. They realize the client is paying for their contributions and they work toward that end. Non work-related time is non-billable time – they keep that to a manageable level.

If you have an interest in considering becoming a consultant, ask yourself these questions:

- What do I possess that someone would be willing to buy?
- Can I market myself, or do I need someone to do that for me?
- Am I well regarded and have an established brand identity, or should I consider joining a firm with an established brand?
- Do I possess the confidence and authenticity to deliver to the pressures and demands of consulting?

Make no mistake, consulting is not easy and is generally a tough transition. It is a different world from that career you grew up in (unless you began your career in consulting).

Another consideration for consulting is what you will do when you're not on a paid assignment. Consultants define this as non-billable bench time. If you are a self-employed consultant, you can use this time to market yourself, but realize the ebb and flow of your compensation. For every hour or every day you are not billing, you are living off of yesterday's earnings. Benefits you used to take for granted, like vacation or sick days, are now unpaid time off and must be thought of more carefully.

If you are working through an established firm, recognize that they will be sharing the client's billings with you. They may or may not be withholding taxes on your behalf. You might not get paid until they have collected the invoice from the client, sometimes 30-45 days after the end of each month. This is referred to as a "paid when paid" practice.

Many firms will require you to sign an employment agreement if you are not operating independently. You will want to consider having your lawyer review it to protect your interest. It is not uncommon to have a non-compete, non-solicitation provision.

Before we move on, let me tell you a story of a good friend, Brad. Brad took early retirement from a quite large financial services firm where he was a very successful senior executive. He had a supporting infrastructure (e.g., administrative, legal, marketing, human resources, accounting) surrounding him. We met several times to discuss his interest in consulting, trying to ensure he knew what to expect. Steve, one of my business partners, made this observation, "Brad, I liken consulting to 'guerilla warfare'. You get parachuted in behind enemy lines and must make do with resources you can discover and procure. Coming from a large corporate culture, you were like a modern army. You had air cover, artillery support, logistics and communications services surrounding you at every step of the way. You were trained, you were fed, and you were motivated. You were rarely alone." Steve was spot on in his comparative analysis! So many people take for granted the natural extensions their organizations provide that when they lose that support network, they are uncomfortable at best; lost and paralyzed at worst. If this is you, be sure to carefully consider how you will adjust.

Chapter Worksheet
Consulting

What would be appealing about consulting as a profession?

What scares me about the consulting profession?

Is consulting a possibility in my future? Whether yes or no, here is my reasoning.

What is my takeaway from this chapter?

Entrepreneurship

"I have not failed. I've just found 10,000 ways that won't work"

~ THOMAS EDISON

According to Paul Reynolds, entrepreneurship scholar and creator of the Global Entrepreneurship Monitor, "By the time they reach their retirement years, half of all working men in the United States probably have a period of self-employment of one or more years; one in four may have engaged in self-employment for six or more years. Participating in a new business creation is a common activity among U.S. workers over the course of their careers." And in recent years it has been documented by scholars such as David Audretsch to be a major driver of economic growth in both the United States and Western Europe. Stevenson defines entrepreneurship as "the pursuit of opportunity without regard to resources currently controlled (Stevenson, 1983)."

In their book, *Small Business, Big Vision: Lessons on How to Dominate Your Market from Self-Made Entrepreneurs Who Did it Right*, Matthew Toren and Adam Toren, profile Mike Michalowicz author of the book titled *The Toilet Paper Entrepreneur*. Mike's advice for entrepreneurs interested in starting a company from the ground up: "First you must know that passion does not guarantee success. But ironically, you will be best served by doing what you are passionate about. Here is the whole trick: Passion brings about persistence and the tendency to stick-to-it, and that determination is ultimately what brings about success. So I encourage any new entrepreneur to start a new business in a field they are passionate about – then stay with it. Listen to the customers (or lack thereof) and adjust. Find out what is working and amplify it; discover what is not working and stop doing it. Systemize everything. Never stop. And then, just then, you might have a shot."

Here is an example to drive this point home. I met a couple, a husband and wife, who chose to invest in a popular hair-cutting business franchise. They didn't have a passion for the business per se, but they did evaluate and investigate a number of successful business franchise models before determining where to apply their investment capital. They concluded that it really didn't matter if they knew the core business. They knew they were operationally sound-minded and could re-act quickly to business conditions as they developed. Over time, the lack of passion overcame them. It became hard to motivate a staff when you couldn't get motivated yourself. Good ideas that would come more naturally to those who had been immersed in and had grown up inside this business were not readily visible to them. They grew tired of the grind and the energy required to make it excel. It became a job that neither of them wanted to stay with long term. They sold the franchise and walked away with a monetary loss, but with a gain in the business lesson they had learned.

Entrepreneurship is about taking risk. Are you willing to do whatever it takes to achieve success? The persistence, the will, the unending determination must come from you. You cannot delegate that responsibility.

Entrepreneurs act while others sit idle. They are the true achievers. They do what needs to be done at the time it needs doing. They see problems as opportunities. They know that if it were easy, all would be doing it. They learn from their failings, mitigate their risk and place small bets continually. As SUN Microsystems co-founder Vinod Khosla stated: "I believe in bumbling around long enough to not give up at things. And eventually success comes your way, because you tried to fail in every possible way, the only way that's left is the successful way, and always, for entrepreneurs, seems to come last. It's so obvious when it comes."

"The most valuable thing you can make is a mistake
– you can't learn anything from being perfect"

~ ADAM OSBORNE

When I was networking with Brian, first introduced to you in the chapter, "Life is a series of intersections," it was obvious he held a passion for an innovative business solution. He knew he had a brief chance to turn his idea into something remarkable. He had surrounded himself with an exceptionally talented team who believed in him and in the idea of growing a company that would deliver unique value-added products and services. While Brian chose to set sail in the country's most difficult economic sea, full of turbulent winds and hurricane conditions, he has shown the mettle and steel resolve needed to overcome the odds of failure. He has listened to his customers and adjusted. He says he is constantly listening, adjusting and systemizing the entire business process.

From the very beginning Brian believed he could build a successful company. He told me the most important thing about being an entrepreneur is doing something you love, because that allows you to better handle the personal risk.

Curious to know how one handles the personal risk of starting a business, Brian said that while that risk is staggering, it is not the worst part. "It is when you begin hiring that the risk becomes real. That's when the fear comes in because not only is it my family and livelihood I've put at risk, but now someone else's." Because of the ethics and morals he holds as a person, the idea of hiring new people was far scarier for Brian.

But fear was not really something he had time for. Brian, along with Dave, his business partner, started a business in perhaps the most uncertain economic time in the history of the American work force. The company began as more and more companies were shuttering or reducing the size of their workforce, but it was at this time that Brian felt the call to action. Brian said, "In order to be a successful entrepreneur you must be willing to take risk. If you are risk averse, the job will be too crippling to take on. But if you are willing to do the hard work, it's well worth it."

Brian made it clear that he owes a great deal of success to his business partner. He stated, "When we started, we had to be very clear with one another what our roles would be. Because we were so small, efficiency was key. There was no time for both of us to work on the same task. We had to trust one another. I had so much to do I could not spend my time worrying about other tasks."

From my findings, their relationship still works the same way today. Because they know each other so well and truly trust one another, they can be much more efficient than if one person attempted to do everything. As a result of their willingness to set expectations and goals for themselves, and their ability to respectfully hold each other accountable, their company has grown quickly. They are steadily receiving new contracts for work and continually expanding their work force.

When things appear most dire, entrepreneurs, those willing to accept the risk, will answer the call and start new businesses. While most people would shy away from these poor economic times and attempt to wait out the storm, entrepreneurs will see the blue ocean in their sights, recognize this as the best time to set sail and will move forward. By doing so, they will put people back to work and instill confidence and belief back in our society. They hit problems head-on and take bold action.

Ask yourself; am I that person? Am I willing and expecting to completely immerse myself into something that's high risk and prone to failure? Know the statistics. First-time entrepreneurs have only an 18% chance of succeeding and entrepreneurs who previously failed have a 20% chance of succeeding, as reported by Paul Gompers, Anna Kovner, Josh Lerner and David Scharfstein in their Harvard Business School Working Paper, "Performance Persistence in Entrepreneurship."

On another note, are you ready to accept an equal partner? Some opportunities are too much for one person to consider. Some people wish to share the workload, responsibilities, credit and profits with another (or others). Will you and your partner(s) measure up to your expected commitment of one another? Not everyone wants to work all day and then spend all of his or her free time studying and worrying about the business. The best time to learn this lesson is before you commit yourself to a partnership. It is imperative that you and your partner(s) agree with how responsibilities will be split and how much time is expected from each so that the load will not be too unbearable for any one partner. Know though, the demands of any new business will be quite challenging and will likely stress any relationship or friendship that exists. Be sure you are in synch with your partner(s) on how hard each of you is willing to work.

I found this little story that drives the point home:

A wealthy entrepreneur was disturbed to see a fisherman sitting idle by his boat. He asked, "Why aren't you out there fishing?"

"I've caught enough fish for today," the fisherman said.

"Why don't you catch more fish than you need?"

Reply: "What would I do with them?"

"You could earn more money and buy a larger boat and all of the things necessary to catch more fish. That would allow you to build your business into a powerhouse. You could have a fleet of boats and many people working for you. And, you would become a very rich man just like me."

"Then what would I do?" asked the fisherman.

"Why, you could sit back and enjoy life."

The fisherman said, "What do you think I'm doing now?"

Will this become you or your business partner(s)? Will you be satisfied to under-perform to your potential? Is this work/life balance or laziness? Is quality of life a priority for you and your partner(s)? Is it important from day one?

What is good for one is not necessarily good for another. Establishing your business will require working long hours and a relentless devotion to it. You will want to invest in self-improvement in order to grow your business. You will constantly seek improvement in yourself and your partner(s) to stay ahead of your competition and make your business the best it can be. Owning your own business is not a part-time job, at least not in the beginning stages, especially if you are the sole owner.

Think all these areas through very carefully early on. Plan for the extreme possibilities and work to mitigate your risks. Budget revenue conservatively, and expenses more heavily. Studies indicate that start-up and ongoing expenses are likely to be more extreme than anticipated. Better to be pleasantly surprised with a profit than to find mounting unexpected losses driving up an unhealthy stress level.

Another consideration, if you are considering a partner, is communications and trust. Strong communications allow for timely course modifications and sea changes as times warrant. Good partnerships, like marriages, are formed on a foundation of communications. Understand how you are going to resolve differences - particularly those of significance. One of our clients is a brother/sister partnership where the brother is 2/3 owner, the sister the remaining 1/3. While settling issues is easy based on ownership shares, the residual impact of not considering fully the minority voice can create divisiveness and have serious long-term consequences. This client has been successful largely because both parties communicate and share their points of view, sometimes with extreme passion. They work hard to protect their family relationship, not letting the business poison what has been built over their lifetime. It hasn't been easy, as both have attested, but the cost of failure is too high to risk.

TRUST. The trust I refer to is not in the sense of theft or wrongdoing, but trust that your business partner will "do the right thing"; that he/she will deliver upon their commitments. Some of the greatest success stories in business startups were as a result of strong trusting partnerships. For instance, **Apple** was established on April 1, 1976 by Steve Jobs, Steve Wozniak, and Ronald Wayne. **Microsoft** began on April 4, 1975, when it was founded by Bill Gates and Paul Allen. **Southwest Airlines** traces its roots to the March 16, 1967 incorporation of **Air Southwest Co.** by Rollin King and Herb Kelleher to provide service within the state of Texas. **HP** incorporated on August 18, 1947, founded by Bill Hewlett and Dave Packard. In each of these examples, the trust established early on was deep and was a critical success factor.

Do new ideas come naturally to you? Over the years I have had several. The handheld portable Breathalyzer was an idea that surfaced in my mind when my first child was born in 1980 and Mothers Against Drunk Drivers was formed. I felt it would be a good way to become self-informed of the dangers of driving while under the influence of alcohol. Unfortunately I dismissed the idea as a liability issue. I was concerned about lawsuits if the device wrongfully registered a low alcohol reading. Other ideas? Around that same time came the idea of Velcro closure for cloth diapers. I was continually concerned about the dangers safety pins posed to infants and rambunctious toddlers. Another? How about cars with brake lights on the front of the car, say the backsides of the side-view mirrors? This would alert someone crossing the street if the oncoming car were braking and intended to stop. How about car tires that visibly alerted the driver to uneven wear and low air pressure? I know - ideas that go unanswered remain dreams. I mention them only to stimulate your creative thinking in an attempt to stay out in front of the innovation curve.

In closing this chapter, let me relay a story that recently began playing out regarding an artisan shop owner. I was contacted through a mutual friend who asked if I would try to help this shop owner, Liz, keep from having to shutter her company. Upon meeting Liz and listening to her story, I could see that she possessed great passion for her work. She had nearly 50 consignors exhibiting their personal creations of art for sale in her shop. She was only slightly in arrears paying her operating expenses, but had not found a recurring revenue stream to offset those costs. Anxiety was high as she had already begun to remove consignments from display and had notified her landlord that she would be closing. Through her words and actions, I felt the gravity and pain of her loss. While we put together a number of "save the store" ideas and programs, we were very late in the game to save her store. I don't know if we will be successful in keeping her dream alive, but it was sobering to realize that despite great passion and a strong work ethic, the flames representing hope, ingenuity and resilient spirit unfortunately can, and sometimes do get extinguished. No one said this would be an easy road.

"Entrepreneurs: The only people who work 80 hour weeks to avoid working 40 hour weeks."

~UNKNOWN

Chapter Worksheet
Entrepreneurship

What are <u>my</u> personal risks toward becoming an entrepreneur?

What franchises would I like to own and operate, or what business would I consider starting?

Would I want a partner? Would I be a great partner?

What is my takeaway from this chapter?

Working in Nonprofit

"Try not to become a man of success but rather try to become a man of values."

~ Albert Einstein

Having volunteered on nonprofit boards and committees for the past 35 years, I can definitely say the experience has shaped me both personally and professionally. I encourage everyone, particularly young professionals, to find their passion for investing in their local community. Writing checks, while critical to meeting the ongoing demands of a nonprofit, does not optimally engage the heart. It's the time investment that pays enormous dividends and will help sculpt the core of the contributor.

As the economy has thrashed and faltered, a number of people have turned to the nonprofit sector for possible employment. I have overheard many say, "How lucky the agency will be to have me." They speak as if the world of nonprofit is comprised of those with inadequate and paltry skills and talent. I can assure you that is not the case. A related myth is that the nonprofit sector is for those who could not make it in the business world and is also far from the truth. In fact, nonprofit organizations employ passionate, highly skilled and intelligent people, many with graduate degrees and meaningful years of experience. I have found that many people are unable to make the transition to nonprofit employment, which often has different and rigorous standards of success.

Private, public and nonprofit sector organizations employ people of all types. There are stresses, personalities, egos, discord and difficult situations everywhere - yes, even in nonprofit. I am reminded of a young person's internship with a large nonprofit. Andy had immersed himself. He was committed to making a positive difference in a world he was sure was filled with good people, good intentions, teamwork, positive spirit and camaraderie. After his first couple of weeks, we met for lunch and he expressed his amazement that the workplace was so aggressive and competitive - more like the places he had worked in the private sector. While I have seen more empathy and care wrapped around the nonprofit sector, each organization is a business and each business has its own path containing struggles and good fortune. With the current economic climate for philanthropic giving bearing a more intense competitiveness and a teetering foundation, it is no wonder their fight for survival has germinated greater stress.

Within their own world, nonprofits are competing with limited resources to advance their brand, relevance, recognition and drive for increased funding. We are most certainly going to see greater collapse and consolidations occurring within this sector as the weaker and less resourceful are plagued to find a survival strategy. All will be driven to squeeze out excess capacity and strive for operational excellence and a more efficient business flow. The burnout factor is certain to rise as the sector is pushed to do even more with less.

Let me relay the story of Kim, a good friend who had been successful throughout her career as a CPA, leader and ultimately a CFO for a major division of a large financial services firm. Kim was reflecting over her career and was wrestling with dramatic change, searching for bliss and greater harmony. As Kim told me her story, she became visibly shaken at describing an awakening she had recently experienced. Despite all the professional success she had accumulated, she felt emptiness, a void. She felt as though she had not returned appropriate value to her community and was evaluating better ways to be personally satisfied yet able to demonstrate improved stewardship. She had refocused her resume on the volunteer and community support she provided. It did a nice job of providing a bridge to her story. She was ultimately successful in securing the job of CFO for a large non-profit that focuses on children, one of her greatest interests. She now radiates great joy and overwhelming satisfaction when discussing her new role. She feels as though she found a gift and is living a dream. I've never found her to be quite so effusive when discussing her career. She is indeed blessed.

Let me introduce you to Melina. Melina has been a dear friend for nearly fifteen years. She has devoted decades of her life to the nonprofit industry. When asked how she first got involved in nonprofit, she captivated me with her story. Her nonprofit history began at the age of seventeen when her parents decided to move to Bangkok, Thailand, and she was forced to go with them. She wasn't excited about the move. Recalling the experience she said, "I left the states a blonde teenage girl, and returned a woman on a mission." What was that mission? To help people in any way she could.

She returned to the States and completed her education. After relocating to Florida, she decided she would begin volunteering at one of the nation's largest nonprofits. She fell in love with the company and became an employee, eventually leading Major Gifts. She has since gone on to lead two other national nonprofits as CEO.

Looking back on her time in nonprofit and her experiences, she encourages one to understand that nonprofit work is not like anything else. On the one hand it is a business with certain goals and deadlines that must be achieved. At the same time, it is the "feel-good" place people think of when they think nonprofit. She suggests, "People should not fear nonprofits operating like a business. As long as you value the individual and - more importantly - value and uphold the cause, operating like a business is not a bad thing. It should increase revenue that you can reinvest into the cause."

Nonprofit employment can be a great reward and provide a sense of great fulfillment. If you have a passion in a particular area or with a specific organization, perhaps you should lean into the opportunity first as a volunteer to ensure your impressions are accurate and the potential value you can offer is in strong alignment with their need. Even if you don't find employment, please consider the values of volunteering!

Chapter Worksheet
Working in Nonprofit

What about nonprofit organizations might I find attractive?

What nonprofit missions am I attracted to?

What is my takeaway from this chapter?

My Attic and the Easter-Egg Hunt

"The future depends on what we do in the present."

~ MAHATMA GANDHI

Having reviewed so many resumes, I have felt at times that my eyes might bleed and I would go numb. I am always amazed at some of the most basic mistakes and failures I find on incomplete or weak resumes. Please pay close attention to these fundamentals:

- Shorter is better - 2 pages, no more than 3 – don't try to meet this limit by reducing the font size! Nothing smaller than a **12 point font**.
- Don't develop your resume using a widely marketed template (Microsoft Word). You want to stand out, be unique, and not look like everyone else! This includes look, fonts and format.
- Don't tell me what responsibilities you held, but what you accomplished with those responsibilities.
- Don't develop your resume as a chronological diary – but a story of progression and advancement.
- Don't make the reader search for nuggets of value. Isolate and highlight them.
- Tailor your resume to the job you want next and build a solid bridge from your personal story to that resume.

During this most recent recessionary period plagued with corporate bankruptcies and jobs lost, I met Bobby. Bobby was a 35-year loyal associate of a large, multi-billion dollar retailer that fell to bankruptcy. One of my opening questions in all networking sessions is, "So, please tell me your story". At this question Bobby silently looked down in contemplation and thought, looked up at me and forlornly responded, "I don't have a story, Mike." I stressed to Bobby that he was going to get one shot, one chance to meet with individuals who might be able to assist him in his quest to find that next job challenge. He needed to be prepared and engaged for those conversations. Your story is developed from a personal introspection. What have I done throughout my career? What do I most enjoy doing? If I wish to transform myself to something new, what proof or credibility have I established to sell that notion? You should establish and exhibit great passion and self-confidence for that story. If you don't believe it, why would anyone else?

I looked over Bobby's resume which was in a similar unprepared state. First, it was twelve pages long! "Bobby, your resume looks like my attic. I'm sure there is something good in here, but you're making me search for it – you're turning it into an Easter-egg hunt."

Like many mature workers, Bobby had held many roles of progressing responsibility over his vast career. He had built a deep and respected technical depth, an established entrepreneur record, and a solid management track. He had highlighted every role and primary responsibility he had ever had. However, it did not stitch together a very compelling story.

"Bobby, why don't you consider separating these twelve pages into three distinct resumes, each with a different theme? One could outline your strength and prowess at assisting new startup opportunities; another could highlight your successful technical career and the final one could emphasize your management background."

It's important to note that I never ask anyone to invent or fabricate anything on their resume, but you should stress those accomplishments you are most proud of and that delivered the greatest benefit to your employer. Even if you were a team contributor, take credit for the business value of the accomplishment – what revenue was generated, what efficiencies were produced, what costs were eliminated, what risks were mitigated or avoided? Write so that you convey a strong business understanding.

On a separate note, when you find yourself out of a job, compose two lists; one list outlining those things you *want* to do, and a second one that defines those things you *can* do (see figure 9). I have encountered individuals who get so focused on what they want to do that even under very stressful conditions (threat of foreclosure, or loss of power or water utilities), they never drop back and seek jobs they are certainly qualified for, but are no longer interested in performing. When it comes to meeting financial obligations and meeting Maslow's basic hierarchy needs, all options should be noted and considered.

Figure 9

Chapter Worksheet
My Attic and the Easter-Egg Hunt

What's my story?

On a scale of one ("I wouldn't hire me!") to five ("I can't believe that's me!"), how would I rate my resume based on what is outlined in this chapter, and why?

What is on my "can do" list?

What is my takeaway from this chapter?

The Real Estate of Your Resume

"Trust yourself. You know more than you
think you do."

~ BENJAMIN SPOCK

Let me start with this important proclamation: **Your resume will not
get you your next position**. If prepared properly, it will get you in the
door. As we discussed in an earlier chapter, your network will prove to
be the most powerful weapon at your disposal.

Think of your resume much like an edition of a good local or big-
city newspaper. The most important space on any newspaper is the
front-page, above the fold. This area of your resume (top-half of first
page) should be your personal headlines. What do you want people
to know most about you? One approach I have introduced to folks is
to identify three adjectives and/or nouns that best describe them and
would fit the types of jobs they are pursuing. Take those three descrip-
tors and center them prominently on a dedicated line (some have en-
hanced the look by italicizing and bolding their appearance).

Examples to enlist your thinking might include:

Negotiator	Analytical
Servant Leader	Fiscally Prudent
Collaborator	Focused
Consensus Builder	Strategic

Quietly Confident	Accountable
Detail Minded	Achiever
Creative	Deliberate
Mentor	Tenacious
Determined	Perseveres

Be careful not to make them sound so nice and soft that you might also describe your pet golden retriever in the same manner!

Let me qualify my next set of comments with the fact that I am a very tough resume critic. Let's start with the first given: **no one but you can set a deadline for when your resume will be ready for distribution.** Given that principle tenet, your resume should be expected to be **without error!** It is arguably one of the best determinants of a person's quality. If errors are present in a product that is this critical, what does it say to imply to a potential employer about your work on the job? Take the time in preparation to ensure it is absolutely perfect. Have a friend or two whose judgment you respect carefully review it and provide tough and honest feedback. If resume preparation is not one of your strong suits, I implore you to invest in an outside professional rendering. While your resume will not guarantee you your next job, you can bet a poor quality resume will eliminate you from consideration. Poor quality can't help you, and it will surely harm you. Take the time to get it right.

I'm often asked about the use of bullets on a resume. Let me offer these basic guidelines for bullets:

- Consider extracting the most salient and powerful accomplishments across your job history (those which align best with your pursuits) and place them as bullets as an executive summary on the first page, above the fold (AKA 'best resume real estate').
- Ensure that all bullets are sequenced and presented by impact in descending order, most powerful first. If I am only going to read the first couple they should be the most impressive and impactful!
- All bullets should be presented in past tense – it's what you did, not what you are doing.
- Limit the number of bullets – the fewer you have, the more impactful they will be.

- Remember to present accomplishments in business terms, e.g., revenue raised, risks mitigated, regulatory requirements met, costs avoided or eliminated. Do not list tasks, roles and responsibilities!
- Be consistent in your use of periods closing each bullet – either they all close with a period, or none do.
- If you use bullets to outline your areas of proficiency, be distinct and succinct. The more of them you have, the less impactful they will be. The less distinction among them, the more cloudy your message. Do not add strengths in areas that would be considered table stakes for the position e.g., budgeting for managers.

If you are considering opening with an objective statement, choose words that are yours. Avoid words that the reader will need to look up in a dictionary. This section should be simple, two or three short sentences, and should aim to convey your interest and next pursuit. It should give the reader a valid glimpse of the person defined by the resume.

The longer your work history, defined by years of service, the less important the early years are in terms of resume detail. The most important years are those defined by your last employer and progression of roles. It will be apparent to you when to simply list the past employer, years of service and job titles you held.

Another common question pertains to the bottom of the last page. What's the best use for that real estate? If you have interests that you might wish to highlight, this would be the place. Examples that deserve attention are civic organizations you belong to, boards and committees you serve on, coaching, teaching and mentoring you provide, charities you are committed to, and alumni associations.

In one related case I was networking and preparing a candidate for an upcoming interview. Ryan pointed out his membership in Mensa. He had highlighted it at the end of his resume and asked me if I thought it was appropriate. "Ryan, this is something you are proud of. It offers an ice-breaker of sorts and recognizes an accomplishment few people possess," I responded. Later, subsequent to his interview, Ryan relayed to me that his interviewer shared the same accomplishment! The entire interview was a little less stressful by that one point in common.

Another time, someone called out his interest in martial arts at the close of his resume. I told him, "David, the fact that you attained the level of black belt reflects your discipline and dedication to your goal. The fact that it was achieved in conjunction with a father-son activity makes it even more defining."

Are you sitting down? I'm going to give you a tip that will leave you shaking your head at its simplicity, yet its power will have you saying, "Wow!"

By now most people are familiar with the term SEO, Search Engine Optimization. Improving the visibility of a website in search engines is critical to improving the success of ecommerce business. SEO is built upon the premise that there are certain keywords or tags, embedded in the programming code that support a particular website/webpage. When these words are entered inside the search box of any particular search engine, like Google, the results are displayed from 'hits' on these key words. What does all this have to do with your resume, you might be wondering. Well, please read on. In many, many cases resumes get entered into applicant tracking systems, knowledge management databases, a repository or a collection of all resumes received over time. If I was looking for a particular candidate, a nuclear biologist with a PhD, I would simply enter those key words into my database search and those applicable resumes would be returned. The challenge is knowing what words you should consider establishing as key word identifiers. The more you have, the busier your resume will look which usually will work against you. Here's the tip:

Using a white font, place key words at the bottom of your resume pages where you have ample white space!

Think this through - no one is likely to print your resume on black paper, but if they do, be proud to explain your desire to stay relevant in searches. As long as you do not invent or fabricate anything in your key words, you can hold your head up at your ingenious approach to being identified. Resume Search Engine Optimization at its finest!

We discussed the possibility that, with an extensively diverse background which perhaps spans many years, you could have multiple resumes. Recall the earlier story of my friend, Bobby. He had enough good career material to compose three distinct resumes. One resume would detail his talents and prowess for establishing new lines of business. A second resume would outline his extensive and vast technical successes. And a third would be used to convey his rich management experience.

However, don't send more than one resume to the same company. I recall encouraging another friend, Tim, to break his resume down in ways that would allow him to present the particular resume that was best suited for the specific job he was pursuing. I even stressed to him that as he focused on a particular position described on the employer's website, he should consider feathering in language that the company used to describe both the position and requirements for the ideal candidate. This subtle enhancement, a just-in-time resume, will generally get a more positive response from the hiring company. And why not, since you're replaying their own language! But what I did not expect was that Tim would send his three distinct resumes (each just-in-time, using the company's advertised language) to the very same human resources recruiter at the very same company!

Rob, a good friend and successful executive, offered a thoughtful counter perspective. "I have altered my point of view on tailored resumes over the last few years. The word 'simplify' comes to mind. I offer this solely as something to contemplate. I know this runs counter to your advice, but I wonder if the tailored resume is the way to go these days. Don't get me wrong, I used to prepare job description-specific resumes regularly and they make intuitive sense. That said, it is so much easier to verify and crosscheck these days with resumes posted online. It is easy to say one thing in one place and something else in another. The simple problem of sending a different resume to the same company online is magnified greatly. I urge everyone to keep consistency and control of the message on paper, online and in-person. Today, that may be best accomplished by keeping it simple."

While Rob makes a valid point, I believe those of us with extensive and varied backgrounds are in the best position to build separate stories tailored to specific job searches. I emphasize this one point – never invent or fabricate anything on your resume. If you are honest, you will never have to apologize to anyone for tailored resumes.

Things to consider in constructing a tailored resume to suit a specific position:

- Compose accomplishments from your career history that best promote you for that advertised role.
- In reading over the job description, characteristics and skills of the ideal candidate, cull out the words and language that resonate with you. Find the appropriate places in your resume to incorporate that same content.
- Reduce or eliminate job material that conflicts with or serves absolutely no benefit to your story.
- Refrain from sending multiple variations of your resume to the same recruiter in the same firm for varying openings (Yes, I have seen this happen!)

Use standard fonts. The most common and effective typefaces for you to consider when preparing your resume (and which are scan-friendly) include Times New Roman, Arial, Helvetica, Verdana and Courier.

A final point on your resume: This is not the time to apply great humility to your story and related accomplishments. Without inventing or fabricating anything, please take requisite credit for the good work that you have amassed over your career. I have had numerous candidates who, after reviewing my objective draft of their resume, have relayed to me, "Wow, I did not know I was that good. I'd like to meet that person some day!"

If this is not your skill, seek outside professional assistance in developing your resume. Allow someone you trust to trumpet on your behalf.

Chapter Worksheet
The Real Estate of Your Resume

What three words best describe me?

On a scale of one ("I wouldn't hire me!") to five ("I can't believe that's me!"), how would I rate myself based on what's outlined in this chapter, and why?

What are the three improvements I intend to make to improve my resume?

What is my takeaway from this chapter?

Section Worksheet
Preparation

What are my top 3 takeaways from this section, Preparation?

-
-
-

Before you proceed to the final section, Execution, I need you to carefully consider what you've learned from Preparation.

> Do you understand the power and benefit of networking? Do you fully commit to networking?
> Do you buy in to the concept of relentless practice?
> Have you examined the companies you are attracted to through your application of Lenses & Filters? Have you ranked them?
> Have you assessed your current resume, applying the tips and techniques from this section? Have you iterated it and improved it? Does it properly bridge to your story? Are you 100% sure it's error-free?

You have performed an intense self-discovery through Reflection. Upon that established foundation, you have laid the knowledge you have gained through Preparation, creating a formidable base to execute from. You know who you are and you have a personal marketing plan. You are now prepared to advance to Execution – Congratulations!

3.Execution

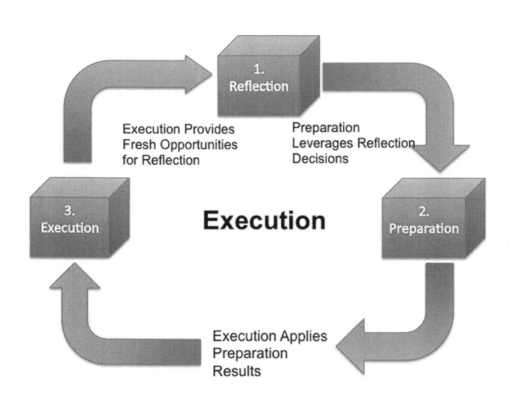

Interview Coaching

"You don't tell me what I want to hear. You tell me what I need to hear."

~ TOM, A RECENT INTERVIEW CANDIDATE

Over the past several years I have experienced an increased demand for my role as interview coach. When the job market is saturated with candidates, it is important that you leave little room for error and do all in your power to be at your absolute best when the time comes for you to interview.

I work closely with candidates to understand their skills, strengths and experience. I suggest mock interviews for candidates who have been out of the job market for a considerable time, or who have an important interview approaching and who want to be best prepared.

Recently, Rod, my business partner, and I invested half a day preparing an executive for an upcoming interview. In advance, we spent several hours combing the website of the hiring company to learn as much as we could about their culture, framework for decisions, priorities and leadership profiles. We composed our interview structure with all this data collected.

Our mock interview was an incredible practice session. Our candidate responded with complete ease and confidence. We did, in fact, make a number of small improvements in his responses such as tone, volume, speed, and pause. Of paramount importance was for him to **be present, be authentic** and **be expressive** as he approached the interview.

During our interview, he missed two questions he had not considered and did not respond with the same ease and confidence he had been exhibiting. But isn't that the purpose of practicing? One question was of a technical nature that was within his area of expertise and the other a more general discussion regarding professional failure. The questions aren't really important. Being best prepared is the goal.

Here is our candidate's take on the coaching: "This was beyond my wildest expectation. While I felt in good control, you asked hard questions and provided great insights on my responses. I know I am better prepared to handle the real interview."

We also provided him with a series of thought-provoking questions to ask during this phase of the interview process. While he had already compiled his own list of questions, he did convey we had a couple that he had not considered.

Subsequent to our coaching and to his interviews with the prospective company, he made this pertinent observation: "You have to really approach interviewing differently than any other form of social interaction. These people don't possess the benefit of knowing you for years and are not aware of all your skills, so if you don't display them, they aren't there."

Here is an exercise to help you prepare for an interview. Take a pad of colorful sticky notes and write questions on them you feel will most certainly be asked (one question per note). Next, spend quiet time reflecting over the projects and successes you have had in your career. Write down an identifying label for each project on a sticky note. Place the notes with the project labels (your successes) across the center of the table. Arrange your interview question notes around the outside (see figure 10). Try to connect each note-question to the best note-success. If you have note-questions without a note-success you will need to reflect on how you will best answer that question should it come up in the interview. To push yourself a bit further, add to your list of note-questions and work hard to use your existing note-successes to answer them. The key in this exercise is to limit the number of successes you will have to keep in mind when responding to the potential interview questions. It will be necessary to have one success that is outside of the work environment; a personal success story. The interview will likely require you to think of a non-work-related example that would answer a question or two.

Additionally, anticipate responding to a question related to your failures. Be comfortable telling this story. Too many times we become weak and struggle with an admission of failure. Embrace your story of failure, but be sure to highlight your learning and the positive action that you took away from it. I recall a time when an interview candidate said he had never failed. It was obvious to me then that the candidate had not considered this question and the potential power of a well thought-out response. Some argue if you have not failed, you have never taken risk or pushed yourself beyond your comfort level.

Angie, my Atlanta-based colleague, offers this insight; "The key question to prepare for is this – Why you? In answering this question, connect your response to their position. Sell yourself by connecting to their company through your accomplishments."

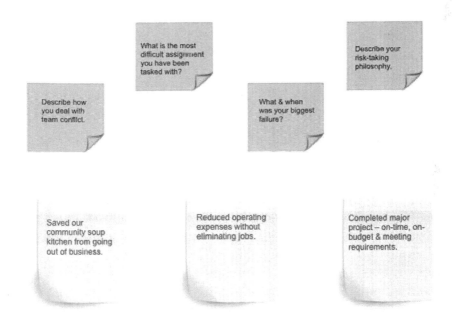

Figure 10

With unemployment for December 2012 at 12.2 million people as reported by the Department of Labor, you would think it would be quite simple to find qualified workers. A survey from Manpower found that 49 percent of companies are having a difficult time recruiting talent despite the abundance of workers available.

Like a personal trainer who pushes you to get real improvements in health and conditioning (e.g., strength, stamina, and flexibility), an interview coach will push you to improve your professional conditioning (e.g., confidence, organized thought, mental acuity and responsiveness).

Make a commitment to improve and get stronger, today!

Chapter Worksheet
Interview Coaching

How could I benefit from an interview coach?

Perform the sticky note exercise. What did I learn from this exercise?

How many successes and how many questions did I develop in the sticky note exercise? Do I find that sufficient?

What failures and learning did I identify for the sticky note exercise?

What is my takeaway from this chapter?

The Dreaded Interview

"Our aspirations are our possibilities."

~ Robert Browning

Some have characterized the emotions of an employment interview like those of heading to the dentist - lots of unknowns and high anxiety. But it doesn't have to be that way at all. When you take control of the process leading up to the interview, you put yourself in a position of strength. Let's begin with your preparation - studying and learning.

Earlier we discussed the lenses and filters to use that provide greater clarity of the firms you are drawn to as potential employers. As you run the overall list of potential companies through your filters, you will gain a qualified list of interesting prospects. An initial assignment for you is to develop a Top 10 list of ideal prospects you consider the Best Bets. **You should mentally protect the top several with an electric fence and razor wire!** This image should tell you to stay out of those companies. Why, you ask? It should be apparent - you are not ready to interview there.

Prepare to interview bottom-up from the list, starting at #10, then at 9,8 and so on until you reach the top tier.

The reason for this bottoms-up approach is rather simple – you are going to make early mistakes. You are going to get better as you climb to the top. Wouldn't you rather improve so that, by the time you reach the top tier of prospect companies, you are at your best? Would you really rather get better as you move downward toward #10? I didn't think so.

Within the preparation area you will need to identify contacts who could provide you with guidance and possible introductions into the interview process. A piece of advice to remember; "Ye shall be known by those you affiliate with." If someone not held in high esteem introduces you into a firm, you run the risk of being characterized in a similar light. Maybe, maybe not, but why run the risk? Use whatever tools you have at your disposal, LinkedIn, friends and family network, websites and search engines, etc., to locate contacts and acquire data intelligence on selected companies.

When you are scheduled for your first interview (hopefully with a lower tier company on your priority list!), It's time to do some critical homework:

- If possible, learn the names of those you will be interviewing with. Once you determine their names, you should look up their background on LinkedIn. Strive to know something about them before walking into the interview.
- Visit their website – carefully review it, locate their news, read up and become familiar with recent happenings.
- Become familiar with their terminology, mission and core values.
- If a public company, locate their two most current annual reports and pay particular attention to the chairman's letter to shareholders.
- List what about the company intrigues you, those things you find appealing.
- List what about the company alarms you, those things you need clarity or confirmation on.
- Determine how much recent change in leadership has occurred.

Also, consider these top reasons why candidates wash out during their interview:

- They show little or no interest – they don't ask questions.
- They speak poorly of their previous employers - they don't take accountability for their performance or actions.
- They deflect criticism – always someone else's fault.

- They fail to "dress for success" – less than inspiring or respectful attire.
- They convey an arrogant, know-it-all, overbearing and over-the-top attitude.
- They are late and unapologetic.
- They have poor body language – little to no eye contact, slumping in seat.
- They have poor language skills – unable to clearly express themselves.
- They exhibit an intense focus on me-me-me (money, vacation, time off, etc.).
- They are not prepared, haven't done their homework and ask mindless questions.

Some important things to keep in mind…

- You are also interviewing them! You are not competing in a beauty contest. Determine if this company deserves you!
- Speak in inclusive terms (e.g., "What will we have accomplished in our first months that will define success in your eyes?").
- Be succinct in your responses. Try to have them do most of the talking. If they want you to elaborate on anything, they will ask.
- Aim to leave them with a sense of mystery about you.
- Dress appropriately for the interview with the company and/ or for the role. You never have to apologize for being over-dressed, but will sure feel awkward from the start if you are not properly attired.

You are also interviewing them. If you were to invest a meaning-ful amount of money, say $1,000, you would surely do a good deal of research and due diligence on the stock or commodity you are consid-ering for investment. That being said, aren't you, and isn't your career, of even more value? In our analogy, most every company would relish your $1,000 investment. Many will find you to be attractive for their job opening. But in both cases, is your $1,000 best placed, and is your career and happiness best served, by making the critical investment decision without the requisite supporting research? Do not fall into the trap of wanting to be liked or accepted by the hiring manager as your top priority. Your top priority should always be: **Does this company deserve me**?

Speak in inclusive terms. When you speak with uncertainty, "if I get this job," or "if I am selected," or "when you make your decision," you provide a subtle point of leverage to the interviewer. They will feel the power of their decision and can sense you are accepting them as decision maker. By taking a more inclusive, outcome-determined approach, you position yourself as more confident and sharing of the hiring decision. Be careful, though, to avoid conveying too strong a message and risk losing any sense of humility and respect. There is a fine line and you don't want to trip over it.

Be succinct. You should strive to leave them wanting more. I've been on both sides of this interviewing point. I have interviewed candidates who did not know how or when to stop talking. I was exhausted at the end of the interview and left feeling there was nothing more to learn, no stone was unturned. On the other side of this point, I have been impressed by the confidence of the candidate to express his response or position with brevity, but also with clarity. The times I wished for more dialogue or expansion of a particular point, I asked for elaboration. Leaving the interviewer with a sense of mystery is an alluring quality, but one to be managed carefully. You don't wish them to think of you as an "empty bucket" or not engaging.

> "Silence is a source of great strength"
>
> ~ Lao Tzu

Fitting attire. My mother reminded me at appropriate times in my development, "If a coat and tie is overdressing, why do folks dress that way when going before a judge, to a funeral, or to an important interview?" I couldn't argue that point. Your attire, like your resume, speaks volume about you and your care for quality. Are your shoes cleaned and polished? Is your shirt laundered and pressed? Are you too flashy or extravagant for this company? Are a dress sweater and nice slacks acceptable? Are people more taken by your dress than by you and your presence? Do your homework and do your best to match your attire with the style and personality of the firm.

Remember to always bring extra copies of your resume along. Invariably you meet more interviewing parties than expected and occasionally some have misplaced your resume.

Shot-gunning resumes with cover letters to firms in a blind fashion is not optimal. First, expect your cover letter to get detached and lost from your resume. If your resume does float around the company, it is not clear where it originated, who owns it, and what position you have an interest in interviewing for.

Getting in the door with a planned and proper entrance improves your chances of success by a large margin. To do this you need to network and build your plan for approach and entry.

In preparing for your interview, consider the range of questions likely to be asked (recall the sticky note exercise from the last chapter). Ask colleagues for good interview questions to help you prepare. Think back to past interviews you've participated in. Here are a number of sample questions to help you:

- Provide an example from previous work experience where you had to solve a problem by thinking and acting outside the box.
- What and when was your biggest failure?
- When have you gone outside your area of responsibility to solve a problem?
- Describe your risk-taking philosophy.
- Describe the values that lead you and that you find non-negotiable.
- Describe how you deal with team conflict.
- What attributes would you use to describe yourself?
- What do you wish your legacy to be? How will you want to be remembered?
- What attributes would you use to describe your ideal work environment?
- What is the most difficult assignment you've been tasked with? What made it difficult?
- Have you ever been called upon to rescue a failed project? What thought process did you use to jumpstart it?
- Who are your heroes, living or dead, that you try to emulate?

- Give me a non-work-related example of when you first began applying business principles.

You can't possibly think of them all, but you can find themes and build a nucleus from your work history to respond to many, if not most. The sticky note exercise described in the last chapter will be a valuable asset to do this. Try to limit the number of projects or work efforts you will need. This will make it easier to respond more quickly and not raise your anxiety level. Keep in mind that the interview is not the place to get too personal. Your responses should be confined to work experiences (except when directed otherwise).

For the last question in my sample list above, I had a good friend relay the following as his answer:

"I recall growing up in a time when many of my friends had paper routes. They would deliver countless newspapers each day, rain or shine, at the same prescribed time. They would also return to each house regularly to collect for their subscription. I had other friends who prepared and sold lemonade on their corner from a small table and chair. I merged the two ideas and came up with this: I took cups of lemonade and put plastic wrap secured with rubber bands on each top and filled the basket of my bike with all the cups. Instead of waiting for people to come to me, I delivered them to areas where people were hard at work and most likely thirsty, such as to construction sites or to people trimming their lawns, walking their pet, or washing their car. I sold out in little time."

The interviewer was amazed at the creativity of this story and it made for a smoother interview. The candidate was later offered the job.

As very few of us would be considered professional interviewers, consider soliciting a friend or co-worker to help you prepare for your interview. I have assisted candidates by running them through a mock interview. I remember a time when Lisa, one of my business partners, joined me to give a candidate, Richard, a trial interview. After a solid hour of peppering questions in a fashion designed to resemble the actual company Richard was going to interview with, my partner abruptly stopped the interview, "Stop," she said. "What's running through your mind right now? You are trying to come up with the perfect answer and you are frequently repeating yourself. You are making it harder than it should be." I told him he was not prepared for the real interview.

After another hour he was more relaxed and a good bit calmer. "Wow, that was really worthwhile." Then he asked, "Can we perhaps do this again tomorrow?"

"Sure," I responded," but not with me. You are too comfortable with me now. I will have another of my partners repeat this simulation with you." We did just that the very next day, and while there was noticeable improvement, he was still not ready for that long day of real-life, when-it-matters, not-a-game set of interviews. Making matters worse, the company he was meeting with was a top-tiered company. He had bypassed the razor wire and electric fence and traipsed right on in. He was not optimal – not at his best – for one of his most coveted companies. Maybe he will improve as he works his way down his list!

When you arrive at the interview, assuming you are in the interviewer's office, look around for ways to build a personal connection. If, for example, there is a picture of the interviewer and his family skiing and you are a skier, you might ask where the picture was taken, note your mutual interest for the sport.

There are two primary reasons you should be prepared to ask questions during your interview. First, it reflects how much time and at what depth you researched the company. It gives your potential employer a sense of your thought process and what's important. Be prepared to respectfully probe. Second, it is your primary purpose to determine if this is the best choice as a potential employer for you. So what questions should you be prepared to ask during your interview? This point I call out now should forever stay etched in your mind – **When you've made the sale, shut it down. If you keep going, only one thing can happen, and it's not good!** This means to pay strict attention to language, questions, length and enjoyment of interviews, along with the myriad of other signals you are sure to be receiving. I have personally changed my hiring decision based on a candidate's incessant need to hear himself talk (more than nervous energy). Your line of questions should be held until the very end unless the interviewer has described a different process. The composition of your questions is a critical part of your interview. Your questions are very telling to the interviewer as to what your focus areas are (remember, it's not about you at this point – no questions about starting pay, vacation, time off, benefits, etc. – not here – not now), and how much detail and intense thought process were put into your preparation and planning. Do not attempt to stump your interviewer with tough technical questions that tout your knowledge and experience. It will be obvious and likely prove detrimental. Do not ask questions that are answered on their website or by material you might have been provided to pre-read. If you are called back for a follow-up interview, your questions should be more probing, as you are beyond the basic understanding of the job. Here are a few sample questions you might consider:

- Now that we have concluded the interview, is there any one thing that still lingers that might indicate I am not your best candidate for the job?
  This question will allow you to close any loose ends or possible misconceptions that exist in the interviewer's mind. You must remain objective and not get defensive at whatever you hear. Stay positive!
- I saw on your website that... (Could be a merger announcement, a new executive hire, corporate earnings, planned growth, etc.) These types of questions reflect your interest in the future of the company and how recent announcements might affect a prosperous future.
- After the first six months you and I have been working together, what will we have accomplished that best defines success?
  This type of question is spoken with an inclusive sense (i.e., I am hired and on board). The spirit of the question is to get an early read on priorities, how aggressive or relaxed the timeframe and deliverable might get projected, and your satisfaction with the work content that gets described.
- I noticed as I was being escorted to your office that everyone appears to be upbeat, happy and engaged. I know that is not an accident. Can you elaborate a bit on the company's culture and how we will work to maintain that positivity?
  Again, try to speak in inclusive terms ("how will *we*"). This question reflects your astute awareness of, and compliments them on, something that is visible and important to you – company culture.
- What key measurements or metrics are we presently using to evaluate the ongoing performance of my area?
  Here you are attempting to discover the degree that metrics are collected and utilized within the company that evaluate and report on progress.

- What have you found to be most enjoyable about working here? Why did you choose this company?
  This brings you closer to the interviewer and conveys a caring, positive message.
- How do you wish to be kept updated as we are working together? Do you have a formal communications process? Do you wish to meet at the close of each day? Do you wish me to seek you out on only important matters? What works best for you?
  This conveys your willingness to adapt to a process in-place and to meet his preferred style for communicating.
- Something has set us apart from the competition. What would you say is our most competitive weapon that promotes winning? This question pays respect to the company's success and is aimed to get your interviewer talking about the differentiator, the "secret sauce."

These are just a sample of questions you might consider broaching in your interview. Select those you are most comfortable asking, and bring your own, those that maybe came to mind as you read over these.

If you are interviewing on site with a potential employer, pay particularly close attention to the company's environment and surroundings. How are people behaving? Is the environment quiet, staid, uplifting, harmonious, inviting, professional? Is it over-the-top in any meaningful way? Can you see yourself fitting in and making an impact? I've seen environments that I would describe as 'library-like', very quiet and purposeful. I've seen others I would liken to an 'adult pajama party' with revelry and behavior that pushed the limits of acceptable business practice.

I recall a time when I had received a job offer from a respectable financial services firm. I told the recruiter who called me with the offer that I couldn't make an informed decision, as I had not been inside the particular building on campus that housed the area under my responsibility. Later that same night, Mike, the CFO, phoned me to ask what more I needed to make my decision. "Mike, I would really like to take thirty minutes and simply walk through the organization to get a feel for its people, culture and spirit." Mike's response was more neutral than anything. I wasn't sure if he was going to pull the offer away, or thought my request was odd, but nonetheless, I deeply cared to see the operation in action. In the end I did take the tour and I recall seeing remarkable energy coupled with vibrant youth throughout the organization. I felt it calling me, as weird as that may sound. But it's true. I felt I could make a difference here.

My message in relaying this story is for you to take an inventory of all that is around you related to the job at hand. Will you fit in? Can you make a difference in a positive way? Is this the place you want to spend the majority of your waking hours for the foreseeable future? Are many of the things you are looking for in that next job present or visible to you? Trust your instincts. If you are receiving negative signals and find the work area to be marginal at best and it doesn't get you excited, pass on it. Allow someone who can check all the boxes of attributes they are looking for take this job. In the long run you will be happier.

Also, know that you will likely be required to interview with 4-8 individuals, probably over multiple days. A number of recent hires have indicated that the days of a single or maybe two or three interviews are behind us. I was recently asked to provide an independent and objective assessment of candidates being considered for a key leadership role for a client. There were probably a total of 6 different interviewers used in an attempt to gain a 360-degree perspective of the candidates. The process ran smoothly and the candidates did not seem to mind at all being herded from interviewer to interviewer. As a matter of fact the candidates used this to their advantage to gain and supplement as much of their own intelligence as possible. They were trying to answer, "Does this company deserve my talent?"

Across the table, company representatives should be trying to gauge a candidate's response to the following central question: *How good is this person at getting things done?* Too often interviewers are enticed more by the education and intellect of job candidates and how well they respond to tough questions. In their book, *Execution – The Discipline of Getting Things Done,* Larry Bossidy and Ram Charan stress that there is little correlation between those who talk a good game, and those who get things done under extreme conditions. They should be looking to select the doer, not the talker. Your job is to ensure they see that you have consistently delivered time and again.

Always be sure to hand write a polite and thankful follow-up note to each interviewing party and be sure to get business cards for correct spelling of names and titles. You might even consider personally delivering them, leaving them with the receptionist, shortly following the interview. This confirms a sense of urgency and strong sense of interest in the position.

Chapter Worksheet
The Dreaded Interview

Taking the list of attractive companies from an earlier Worksheet, who are my key contacts for those companies?

What are my "go to" questions for each of my interviews?

On a scale of one ("I wouldn't hire me!") to five ("I am extremely confident!"), how would I rate myself based on what's outlined in this chapter, and why?

What are the three improvements I intend to make to improve my interviewing?

What is my takeaway from this chapter?

Follow-up and Next Steps

"Those people blessed with the most talent don't necessarily outperform everyone else. It's the people with follow-through who excel."

-MARY KAY ASH

As soon as the interview is behind you, you have a wonderful time to reflect on both the positives and the negatives, all while it is fresh in your mind. As a reminder, don't forget to send a personal, hand-written thank you note to each of the parties you interviewed with. Do this within 48 hours of your interview. This little consideration will never harm you and might actually be the tipping point for you getting the job offer.

But what if you don't get the job offer? What if you never receive any notification? Sadly, this does occur more times than I like to witness. You deserve to hear something, positive or not.

Some interview candidates seem to become paralyzed and do absolutely nothing to follow up on an interview. They sometimes fear the actual fear of rejection. "If I never find out I wasn't selected, maybe I'm still in the running." Staying in touch with the company is important. Even if you were not selected for this position, staying close with the hiring manager, human resources contact or your recruiter may prove valuable later when other positions become available. It is also important that you grade or rate yourself immediately after each interview.

Discuss your evaluation with an objective third-party, e.g., an advisor, mentor or coach. Factor their feedback into future interviews.

So, how did you close the interview? Did you ask about the process and what the next steps would be? Did you ask when you might hear something? Did you ask when you should follow up? Don't be incessant by calling every day or several times each day. Using the timeframe provided to you, make your call soon after the prescribed deadline. If the deadline was extended, reset your follow-up date. You might also ask if there is anything else they might need from you to aid in their decision-making. While it should be obvious, I will say it anyway – do not come across as desperate. Remain upbeat and positive. Have a little lilt in your voice that projects respect and confidence.

You should also give consideration to the fact that prospective employers may be calling references and performing other background checks per company protocol. In this, the Age of the Internet, it is becoming more common than not for employers to search social media sites to learn as much as possible about their finalists under consideration. We are all aware of stories of people losing their jobs because of online pictures or tweets depicting inappropriate behavior. Examples include a teacher who was on summer vacation posing for a relaxing picture with a beer hoisted above her head, or the recent tweet from the athlete from Greece who was dismissed from her Olympic team for an off-color tweet. Some prospective employers are asking candidates to sign onto their personal sites so that they may review them.

I recall an undergraduate course in ethics where the professor entered the classroom on the first day with a handful of papers. He looked at the papers and looked over the class, repeating this exercise for effect. He then called out several names of students in the class and informed them of how much publicly available information he was able to procure from simply searching the Internet. Much of the material gathered was embarrassing for the students within the guise of that environment. He simply asked the students to consider how this information would serve them as they began to embark upon a professional career. No other generation before them has had to endure this level of scrutiny or availability and immediacy of information.

Using any Internet search engine, search your name. Anything come up? Is your LinkedIn profile current, up-to-date and relevant?

In light of the most recent economic stress, with foreclosures, delinquencies and bankruptcies running high, candidates must concern themselves with the accuracy and quality of their credit report. I recently had the privilege of presenting a stellar executive candidate to a key leadership role with a large regional financial services firm. All lights were green; all systems go - until the credit check was processed. My candidate had gone away on a planned vacation and was caught having to straighten out many hiring questions and discrepancies from a faraway location. Fortunately this story had a happy ending, but not all will be so fortunate. You can avoid much of this if you are proactive and have kept your history accurate and current.

Chapter Worksheet
Follow-up and Next Steps

What three things will I do after each interview?

What is my takeaway from this chapter?

Section Worksheet
Execution

What are my top 3 takeaways from this section, Execution?

-
-
-

Congratulations!

As outlined in Figure 11, you have completed the arduous task of Career Planning. More than that, you have engaged in a process of life discovery. You have shed your doubts, veils of pretense and any negative and paralyzing emotions brought on by the pressures related to your job search.

You have a renewed sense of purpose, a refined self-image and a much improved action plan. You now understand the importance of the steps within the Career Planning Model. You understand the sequencing as outlined by the model.

Reflection took you out of your comfort zone, urging you to refocus your energies in a more positive way, understanding happiness and expressing gratitude and an abundance for life. You affirmed your personal values, finding those things most critical to your career search.

Preparation expounded the power of your networking. Through lenses and filters, you discovered factors critical to finding your next job opportunity. You found the principles of practicing to improve your confidence, enhance your story, and tighten your clarity around critical job factors. You learned much more about the power of your resume and it's bridge to your story.

Execution brought it all together. You are able to attack your search with more directed energy and more confidence. You know that the central question to ask in each interview is, "Do they deserve my talent?" From here, we'll put a bow around the process and discuss some behaviors and observations that have been occurring and growing within the job market. Consider this your cool-down from a very long run. Soak it in and enjoy these final chapters!

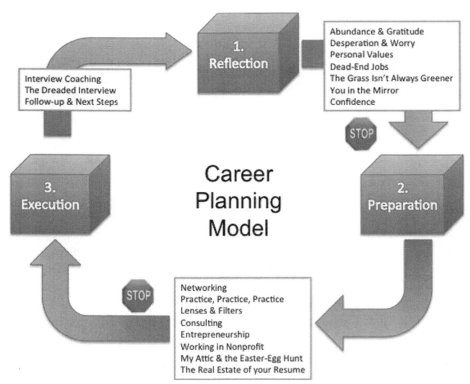

Figure 11

Loyalty – A Thing of the Past

"Loyalty is dead, the experts proclaim, and the
statistics seem to bear them out. On average, U.S.
corporations now lose half their customers in
five years, half their employees in four, and half
their investors in less than one. We seem to face
a future in which the only business relationships
will be opportunistic transactions between virtual
strangers."

~ FREDERICK F. REICHHELD

As I have travelled through the many years of my career journey, I
invariably met co-workers who had invested most of their lives,
certainly much of their career, with a single firm. It just wasn't unusual
to find large pockets of dedicated and loyal workers who devoted
their time, without so much as a question of doubt, to one company.
It seemed to work both ways. Firms were careful to protect the tribal
knowledge possessed by their workforce. Experience won out over the
less tenured. I can recall my elders, those people I respected, telling me,
"Things aren't like they used to be when we were young." Boy, were
they right! Loyalty is no longer rewarded. Quite the opposite. Stay too
long in one place and your market value actually drops. Stay too long
in one place and the powers above will circle like buzzards, waiting
for you to quit or get terminated. Please don't mistake my point with

entitlement. I do not believe we have a forever right to that job. I believe we have to earn our jobs each and every day. But loyalty has become a diminished quality, not one to be cherished. Stay too long and people will invariably ask, "Can't find something else? Not motivated to grow? You don't owe them anything. Scared to move on?"

Over recent years, which have been compounded by the troubled economy, weak job market, high foreclosures in the housing market, and the shocking elimination of jobs with people performing at or above average skill, my position on loyalty has shifted. I now stress that you are to be loyal to only one – You. Be loyal to yourself and to your family. Protect and provide for them. If you are offered a job with a company, perhaps not in your primary tier and not on your "want to do" list, but which falls squarely on your "can do" list, you may be inclined to accept it to maintain your place as a provider for your family. Hold your head up and accept it if you are becoming overly worried or desperate. Even if you continue to look for a better job, it is much easier to find a job while employed. I will also urge you to really consider this new role. You might actually find you like it and want to stay. That can and does happen. Not a bad outcome for either you or the company. Both of you share the obligation to create a positive work environment. Both of you should be giving to the other, and maybe, just maybe, things will work out for a longer term.

Lesson Learned?

"It is easy -- terribly easy -- to shake a man's faith in himself. To take advantage of that to break a man's spirit is devil's work."

~ GEORGE BERNARD SHAW

During the recent collapse of the job market, an emergence of abhorrent corporate hiring practices appeared. Companies suddenly were more carefully and stringently evaluating candidates for hire. During better times, these same companies would gladly accept candidates who possessed 8 of the 10 requirements for the job. Now, however, companies passed on these candidates saying, "We elect to keep looking for the candidate who meets all of our requirements." What was often not considered was the opportunity cost of delaying the hire and appreciating the fact that the candidate who met 8 of the 10 requirements (and who they often liked, by the way) could possibly pick up the remaining two requirements while on the job. These delays, while searching for the ideal candidate, often lasted six to eight weeks. Companies were caught up in the ever-growing pool of exceptional unemployed talent, thinking that if they waited long enough, the absolute perfect candidate would appear. Unfortunately, they continued to believe that the longer they waited, the better their chances were in landing Mr. or Ms. Perfect. A vicious negative cycle emerged and was perpetuated.

One additional point to ponder from the residue left behind from this behavior is the employer's commitment to associate training and development. Is this a sign that employers are removing themselves from responsibility for the continued growth and betterment of their workforce? It seems portentous that they are expecting their new hires to come completely ready to work.

Another repugnant behavior seen during this same time was low-balling the offer amount by applying leverage against the unemployed candidate, thinking they would be forced to accept the low offer to care for and protect their family. More times than not, they were right. Candidates frequently lowered their expected salary to make them-selves more attractive. Sounds an awful lot like the housing market doesn't it? I don't mean competitive negotiations resulting in a drop of a few thousand dollars. It was not unusual to see more than twenty thousand dollars being pulled back from the offer.

A few key points were missed by this behavior. First, those can-didates who felt coerced and taken advantage of were often the first to leave that job when the job market improved and more job oppor-tunities were available. Who could blame them? There was very little (none?) loyalty to those companies. Perhaps an even bigger point was the message these hiring companies were sending to all the candi-dates during this most difficult time. They were not looking to create a win-win situation. It certainly wasn't leading with a considerate and thoughtful nature. They were perceived as non-caring, self-important and duplicitous. I'm often reminded of a fitting phrase that well de-scribes this conduct – *success hides a lot of sins*. When times are good, people can hide behind their success and pretend they are a company to be admired. But it is during the most difficult of times that actions speak volumes and true colors are in full view.

As we have begun to see visible signs of economic improvement, particularly in the job market for technical skills, the pendulum has swung back to the candidate. Strong candidates are moving quickly and for salaries much more commensurate with their background and skills.

Use this section of the book to consider companies you admire, and why. Examine those that perhaps have not performed admirably dur-ing tough times. You might even wish to use this analysis in the lenses and filters section of your personal marketing plan. After all, we all strive to invest in the best companies, and what a better time to collect current data than during this most difficult period in our employment history?

Many suggest this to be a difficult time for all employers, employees, candidates and suppliers. I find the times to be quite interesting. We see separation between the strong and the weak. How people behave during tough times tells me more about their character, integrity and values than during the really good years. As I said earlier, and it's worth repeating here, *success hides a lot of sins*. Tough times display the truth for all to witness.

Today's Youth is Our Future

"I believe the children are our future. Teach them
well and let them lead the way."

~GEORGE BENSON

Mark, a good and long-time friend, asked if I would meet with his
son, Cory, to help him network and prepare for upcoming interviews,
and offer guidance to his career thoughts. Cory executed flawlessly
against the bullet points outlined in this chapter. He fell easily into my
category, "bright, confident young minds."

Cory's dad is a very successful executive and had encouraged Cory
to consider joining him in the company. Cory, on the other hand, wanted to 'be his own man', make a name for himself and not be influenced
by his dad's good reputation and success. I was impressed with Cory's
confidence and determination to find his own career. I helped Cory
prepare for several interviews using the same techniques I've outlined
throughout this book. I assisted Cory in negotiating the offer he might
receive, giving him a number of things to focus on (e.g., travel, benefits,
education reimbursement, willingness to relocate, future path for advancement, and the corporate culture). He ultimately received an offer
from a company that was not his primary target, but on a lower tier. He
vacillated as to whether to accept the offer, put them off as he waited
for his primary target to respond, or risk declining this one and maybe
never getting the preferred job offer. In the end, Cory accepted the position and shortly afterward was offered a role with the company that

was his primary interest. Perplexed and uncertain, facing a difficult decision, Cory agonized over how to respond. He ultimately elected to withdraw his acceptance from the first company and said yes to the second, his primary target. This proved to be a very difficult life lesson for Cory, quite early in his young career.

I caught up with Cory over lunch recently. He was recruited away from his first job, is returning closer to home, has recently married and is set for great things in his career. His confidence and mental acuity have only gotten better since we first met. He relayed to me, "I think back to our early times together. While I thought I was ready in most regards, I can now see big improvements today over those times. I was so unsure of what I wanted. It seems like so long ago. I am very happy with where I am now. I appreciate all of your support and guidance." Yes, Cory's star shines bright. He's making it.

On my travels to different universities I have visited and met with numerous young people who are graduating or have graduated. I have mixed feelings as to their preparedness to tackle the professional world. I have had the privilege of networking with some of the brightest young minds one could ever hope to meet. They have compiled a meaningful array of accomplishments, including internships, community and charitable volunteerism, awards, clubs, travels and other recognition. They best display a passion and a certainty to their future. Their story rings with optimism and confidence. From and through them I hold high hopes for wonderful accomplishments that are sure to challenge conventional thinking and will undoubtedly change the world we know for the better.

At the other end of the spectrum are those that are not equipped, who have not practiced telling their story, and have not bridged their story to their resume. Their confidence is shallow. They are often confused and in need of direction. This is a population that desperately needs our help and attention.

This latter group, those with resounding doubt and uncertainty, are not unlike the well-seasoned, aging population of workers now being displaced with an ever-increasing frequency. The commonality between the two groups is startlingly similar. It includes:

- Lack of networking experience (or atrophy has set in)
- Low confidence and self-esteem
- Uncertainty of pursuit – where they wish to aim

- Weak or nonexistent story
- Resume fraught with holes, gaps and errors
- No bridge between the resume and their story
- Interviewing skills have withered or are severely limited
- Pessimism overrides optimism – they see a giant obstacle before them
- Lack of organization, planning and self-disciplining skills
- Unsure of where to start, so they either don't or delay and move without a sense of urgency

A number of potential employers have shared with me the following characteristics and behaviors they look for when interviewing young professionals. Here they are in no particular order:

- Be positive and optimistic
- Know your qualities, achievements and talents
- Share your passions
- Come prepared to ask questions
- Seek a balance between social skills and a seriousness and purposeful nature
- Show your intelligence and that you are a quick study
- Display your level of maturity
- Convey your ability to be a team player
- Understand and present your fit with the corporate culture
- Illustrate your leadership potential
- If you're on time, you're late – plan to arrive 10 minutes early (you never have to apologize for being early!)
- Dress appropriately for the organization (shoes polished, shirt clean and pressed?)
- Make sure all mobile devices are silent or are on vibrate only (preferably off)
- Speak up – speak clearly – be heard
- Speak with confidence, but be humble
- Maintain eye contact and listen intently
- Deliver a firm handshake (with eye contact)
- Maintain strong posture (don't slouch!)
- Toss the chewing gum before you go in (not afterwards!)

Let's be sure to find ways to help these young people get the start they need. It will pay enormous dividends and will position our future workforce to do good work. I ran across a quotation recently that caused me pause and reflection – "I must understand, and act on the understanding, that every child is *my* child. Like it or not, the children of our community are a shared responsibility."

"On Your Mark...RUN!"

We've come a long way, my friend. But what you do next will define you and the value you received from our journey together. You may need time to reflect further on the points you've taken away, on the stories that left their mark upon you. You may wish to re-read all or a portion of the material again. That's ok. Do it. Build the muscle to excel, to be at your best.

If you need more motivation and inspiration, let me suggest that you visit the online TED website, www.ted.com/talks and watch a few selected talks (you will also find these talks on YouTube). TED, which is an acronym for Technology, Entertainment and Design, was founded in 1984 in Silicon Valley as a one off event and has grown immensely ever since. They address a wide range of topics, often through storytelling. The speakers are given a maximum of 18 minutes to present their ideas in the most innovative and engaging ways they can. Past presenters include Colin Powell, Bill Clinton, Jane Goodall, Malcolm Gladwell, Al Gore, Bill Gates, and many Nobel Prize winners. TED talks have been watched over one billion times worldwide. Within the Top 20 most viewed talks here are some of my favorites:

1. Sir Ken Robinson: Do Schools Kill Creativity?
2. Jill Bolte Taylor: How It Feels to Have a Stroke.
3. Tony Robbins: Why We Do What We Do.
4. Simon Sinek: How Great Leaders Inspire Action.
5. Steve Jobs' 2005 Stanford Commencement Address.
6. Brene Brown: The Power of Vulnerability.
7. Dan Pink: The Puzzle of Motivation.
8. Elizabeth Gilbert: Your Elusive Creative Genius.
9. Dan Gilbert: Why are we happy? Why aren't we happy?

As I have said to just about everyone I network with, the only voice that matters is your own. You can certainly flush the stories and ideas brought forth from this book. I can attest that the ideas work, but you have to be willing to make one more sizeable investment. You have to commit to taking action, becoming disciplined and organized, and holding yourself accountable for the results. We've run together, making longer and longer runs as we've gone deeper and deeper within the book. The time is now for your best run. You are well prepared and simply need to execute on what you have learned.

Recall the development of your Personal Marketing Plan. Bring forth the lenses and filters you will use to evaluate and approve potential employers. Using data available from multiple sources, e.g., Internet, Chamber of Commerce, local community resources, as well as your own collection of potential employers, cull, qualify and reduce your list to an initial best ten. Keeping focused on your drivers and motivators, rank this list, forming your personal top ten.

It's very important that you refrain from working this list from the top to the bottom. Remember, you are going to improve and get better with each interview. You don't want to gain confidence as you work your way *down* the list! Work from the bottom to the top. By the time you get to the top tier of companies, you will be at your absolute best. Let me point out that some of you may not need to begin at the very bottom. You may be perfectly content to start somewhere in the middle or closer to the top. What's really imperative is that you get some practice with companies you are willing to take more risk with, perhaps even failing to meet your expectations.

Prepare to practice! Prepare to immerse yourself in preparation and trials. Work your story. Bridge your story to your resume. Perfect your resume. Attest to its quality. Make it the best it can be. Be proud of it.

With your top ten list in hand, you need to research to uncover how many people you know in each company and who is most able to get you an introduction.

You need to gather intelligence and learn as much as you can about each company on your list. At a minimum, visit their corporate website and print off the two most recent annual reports. Pay careful attention to the chairman's letter to shareholders. This letter is most often found at the beginning of the annual report. It's here that the list of accomplishments and challenges are outlined and in some cases detailed. The reason you want to review the past two years is to look for consistency within the reports and what lingering issues may be hanging around. Determine if you can see yourself making a difference here.

As opportunities emerge, get your story and resume bridged and tailored to each specific interview with each company. Know how you are going to make a difference. Remember to be brief and succinct. Be prepared to ask probing and well thought-out questions. Stay engaged and leave them wanting more, leave them with a sense of mystery. Know when to shut it down if you feel as though you've made the sale. Bad things occur if you keep going!

Stay confident and optimistic. Remember, you are interviewing them. The real question at hand is, "Do they deserve me?" Can you envision yourself making your mark and leaving a legacy there? Is there a good chance for a solid return on your investment?

Confidence and humility are very important. You have to realize you will get but one chance to make your impression. Make it count.

Don't allow desperation to enter your mind. Be sure to keep both lists updated and close by your side: what you want to do, and what you can do. If time pressures mount, you might have to fall back and focus on jobs not on your want to do list, but where you have a strong history of performance.

Keep networking! Make a point to set a weekly goal to meet a certain number of new people. The math is explosive. If you meet three new people the first week, and if they each give you three new contacts, it will not be long before you will have to expand your callings in an attempt to keep up.

Recall my introduction of Gail from the Confidence chapter. She was awakened at 2:00 a.m. the morning following her termination and she went right to work. She outlined her many skills and gained confidence when she saw that they are not industry specific – she has many transferrable talents. She then set out to organize her contacts and in a very short while had identified 100 people she could reach out to for support and guidance. She lost no time, organized her thoughts and developed an action plan. She hit the ground running. Her traction was moving her forward. She was not getting stuck looking at her immediate past. She went so far as to say, "I am going to be the role model for displacement." Her positive attitude is remarkable! Let it be yours and embrace this time of crisis. The choice is yours.

Depending on your confidence level and how long it has been since you last interviewed, you might wish to seek an interview coach.

Having someone throw you batting practice, hit you ground balls and push you through practice will serve you well. You will sharpen your skills and raise your confidence.

I implore you not to let a week go by that you have nothing to report. Like going to the gym, when you stop for a week you lose muscle, your energy wanes, and bad habits can emerge. Don't allow that to happen. Stay the course. Stay committed. It might help to find a 'workout partner' someone who also happens to be looking for his or her next career opportunity. Push each other and don't allow the other to fail. Encourage each other. After each interview critique yourself. Talk it out with your partner. How could you have improved? You and your partner will learn more from each other's experience than from just yours alone.

When you succeed in landing your next job, remember to retain all the information you have accumulated. Keep the process alive. Keep your networking muscles toned and in good shape. Above all else, make a personal commitment to help others as they reach out to you. You will have some rich personal experience to share. Consider paying it forward. Most importantly, *enjoy the journey!*

Epilogue

You have to leave the city of your comfort and go into the wilderness of your intuition. What you'll discover will be wonderful. What you'll discover is yourself.

~ALAN ALDA

Love after Love by Derek Walcott
The time will come
when, with elation,
you will greet yourself arriving
at your own door, in your own mirror
and each will smile at the other's welcome,
and say, sit here. Eat.
You will love again the stranger who was your self.
Give wine. Give bread. Give back your heart
to itself, to the stranger who has honored you
all your life, whom you ignored
for another, who knows you by heart.
Take down the love letters from the bookshelf,
the photographs, the desperate notes,
peel your own image from the mirror.
Sit. Feast on your life.

Dr. Jean Gasen, a close personal friend, provided me with a copy of Derek Walcott's classic poem, *Love after Love*. She suggested that this poem might be an appropriate point for reflection. For me, the story-line describes life's journey ("the time will come") of self-discovery, being lost and reuniting with your true identity ("you will greet yourself at your own door"), an identity concealed by an ego you fed ("whom you ignored for another"). "Feasting on your life" defines your personal journey of Reflection outlined in this book; your good times ("love letters from the bookshelf"), your revelations ("the photographs") and your pain ("the desperate notes"). I ask you to read this several times, allowing it to sink deep into your core. I believe you will continually gain from it the more times you read it. I certainly have.

If I may be maudlin for just a moment, it is my sincere hope that you discovered something of interest as you read this book. As I mentioned very early on, it was never my intention to write this book; but, once I began, I found it flowed like a meandering river, taking me on my own journey of career and networking memories. I realized I couldn't recall them all, but I hope what I was able to reconstruct and cobble together brought you some understanding and enjoyment.

I have had the immense pleasure, even as I was writing this book, to be stopped and thanked for my assistance by someone who found a new job after we networked and improved some part or all of their story, resume, interviewing, networking, confidence or lenses and filters. Many others have written notes upon reflection of the value they received from our time together. Each note, or personal call or visit is meaningful and will be long remembered and personally treasured. I can tell you it has been a true joy to work with each and every person that I was connected with. Life is indeed a series of intersections and I am profoundly richer by paying close attention to these intersecting times.

If there is one thing I beg of you to take away from this book, it's a commitment to serving and assisting the needs of others. If we each make an effort to help others expand their network, improve their capabilities and confidence to tell their story, pursue new opportunities, and compress the time it takes to find the right job, we can have a dramatic effect on unemployment. It is said that it takes a community to raise a child. We are all children in some sense and we need the support of one another. The next time that phone rings, when that call comes, answer it, "Hello old friend, how can I help you?"

If you are inclined to want to reach out and let me know your thoughts regarding the messages and framework outlined in my book, please email me at info@hellooldfriend.org.

Acknowledgments

There are many people to thank when reflecting over this book-writing journey. It was first discussed back in early 2010 when I was coaching and counseling 6-8 people a week about job and career opportunities. **Lisa Spenik**, a senior business associate, sat through countless sessions with me and observed, "You really need to get these stories out more broadly – they are really good and more people need to hear them." Thank you, Lisa, for your encouraging words.

My wonderful wife, **Julie**, who I first exposed my earliest draft to, was a much-needed beacon of support. A voracious reader herself, she was overwhelmingly supportive of the story being told. Little did she know then, I needed validation. I was desperate for a little glimmer of light to shine over this product. She brought the full sun! Thanks, honey.

Mike Paulette, a retired bank executive, current business partner and a long-time good friend, provided ongoing diligence to reviewing drafts of the book and suggesting many strong and subtle improvements. Mike, I can't thank you enough for your unending support. You helped make this book the best it could possibly be.

Rick Rusin, a good friend I have gotten to know better over the past several years, pushed me, encouraged me, challenged me and provided sound advice and counsel that made the book tighter and better overall. His encouragement in the late hours provided needed fuel for the finish. Thanks, Rick.

Marilyn Anderson, a recently retired business professional, proved to be a godsend as my trusted editor. Marilyn continually amazed me with her discoveries and command of the written word. I am deeply humbled by her talent and blessed through our life intersection, both from a personal perspective and at such a critical time in this book's development. Thank you, Marilyn, for your tireless dedication and for joining me on this journey.

Andy Stevens, a recent college graduate hired by our firm to lead communications and branding, provided strength to this product through his tireless editing and encouragement. He also shared his own journey with you, reflecting on the personal value of this book's content. Andy, thank you for providing the professional style the book sorely needed. Well done, my friend.

Brian Leach, co-founder, president and CEO of Unboxed Technology, but more than that, he is a dear friend and we are huge believers in each other. Brian offered sound advice and constructive edits along the journey and was the force behind the book's cover. The words, "thank you", seem so insufficient, Brian. I am humbled by your willingness to contribute, engage and support this effort. Your words in this book's Foreword are humbling and touch my core.

Dawn Sallas, visual designer for Unboxed Technology, is the creative genius behind the book cover. She captures the essence of life's intersections, and with the individual's shadow looming tall before him, forces a symbiotic relationship to his reflection. The question remains – "who is that I see?" Dawn, your talent and ability to represent the real bones of this book are amazing. Thank you!

Sydney Petty, a long-time friend who lives an attitude of gratitude and brings much joy to those around her. She provided much sound advice and made this book a better product. She also introduced the documentary, *Jiro's Dream of Sushi*, to me. Thank you, Syd, for your friendship and continued support.

Jim Wilson, a retired bank executive, now successful motivational coach, and long-time friend, provided good thought and encouragement. Jim suggested the topic of Abundance and Gratitude be the start of Reflection. I found his suggestion to be quite insightful and on point. I don't think the book would flow the same without it. Thank you, Jim.

Melina Davis-Martin and **Mary Beth McIntire** for their support and voices of relevance. They too felt the storyline and material was pertinent to so many in need. Their guidance, direction and encouragement are greatly appreciated. Thank you!

My fellow business owners at Core Consulting, **Monty Blizard, Don Kierson,** and **Steve Lux**, for their support and unwavering adherence to strong company values. This book parallels the model of caring and service to others that we at Core foster and strive to protect. I truly appreciate your resolute support and guidance.

Several of my teammates at Core Consulting, **Christine Roberts**, **Coates Carter**, and **Rod DeBord**, for their reviews and for filling in the gaps of elements of my stories I had overlooked or failed to properly elaborate upon. You guys saw around corners and recalled stories I had not brought forth. Thank you, all.

Doug Poynter, vice president with the national outplacement and career development firm, Lee Hecht Harrison, has been very kind to include me in his networking of strong, highly skilled, yet unemployed professionals. These interactions have provided numerous life intersections to hone the messages detailed in this book. Doug has been a friend to many in need. Thanks, Doug.

My Choir of Contributors and Supporters; those of you who volunteered to read an early draft and provide encouragement, feedback, insights and suggestions. **Matt Aprahamian, Andy Birken, Kirk Bonner, Angie Chattin, Bill Cimino, Bill Clymer, Al Davis, Tracy Driskill, Dave Egbert, Steve Fletcher, Dick Fortier, Cheri Zeeb-Foss, Michael Foster, Steve Fox, Larry Garcia, Paul Gee, Timberlee Grove, Brenna Haley, Jim Hall, Lisa Hollier, Chris Jones, Kerry Jones, Kim Jones, Don Kierson, Tim Kisner, Donnie Knowlson, Rick Losco, Melina Davis-Martin, Rick Mears, Laura Meloy, Mike Mendelson, Debbie Minix, Curtis Monk, David Nelms, Lloyd Osgood, David Park, Jody Rood, Lyall Shank, Rob Simms, Barbara Couto-Sipe, Chip Smith, Paul Springman, Gregg Sutfin, Jane Taft, Sandra Taylor, Dan Tierney** and **Rob Todd.** You all brought fresh ideas and observations that served to make this a much better product. Thank you for your commitment, support and friendship.

A special thanks to **Sam Jarrar** and his wife, **Allison**, owners of The Daily Grind Coffee House & Café. Many of my life intersections occurred here that have been outlined in this book. So many of these stories claim their roots within the walls of this warm and relaxing café.

Mike Samuel, general manager of a Richmond, Virginia Panera Bread, has been most gracious and supportive of community networking. Many life intersections take place here each and every day.

To all whose experiences have been shared, please know that without you, these stories would never have been told. I hope our life's intersections brought you some value, security and solace. Thank you all for allowing me to intersect with your journey. I hope you enjoy finding your piece of the story within these covers.

Afterword

Please allow me to introduce myself. My name is Andy Stevens. I am a recent college graduate who was awarded the unique and humbling opportunity to help edit Mike's book and to interview a number of people who had networked with Mike over the years. Mike has applied his framework, raw and unwritten, to many, many individuals. I wanted to personally test the process in parallel to the outline of this book. Over the course of doing so, I found in my own reflection, the need to apply the framework for my own personal journey. What follows is my journey along with related stories from my interviews with others who have collided with Mike in one of his "life's intersections".

It was March of 2011. I had the opportunity to network with Mike Jones. Through a series of serendipitous events, Mike and I met and began a professional mentorship that continues today. I was in my final undergraduate year of college when I first received coaching from Mike. To say I was ill prepared to join the workforce when I met Mike is an understatement. I was a shy, neurotic individual terrified I wouldn't find work. I had no idea of my strengths, or how to present them to others, and I was so scared of not finding work I reeked of desperation in interviews. It's not that I wasn't trying. I went to every career fair, on campus interview, and networking event to which I could obtain an invite, but I had no plan or strategy behind those actions. I was merely shot-gunning resumes to any and everyone who had mailboxes, and had no idea how to use my strengths to my advantage.

I had no real work experience to speak of when I was first introduced to Mike. I had been a waiter for a time, processed fulfillment in a national shipping warehouse, worked as an assistant through a work study program, and even worked as a custodian for a gas station, but had no idea how to translate those jobs into marketable skills for a career. Like all college students, I wanted to position myself in the best possible place to get a job after school, but I was clueless. I reached out to Mike for guidance, and after a few meetings he sent me down the path this book follows.

When I was nearing graduation, and getting more and more nervous. I was scared I wouldn't find work, and a bit frustrated that the path Mike and I had traveled down had not translated into any positions with any companies. Mike took me out to lunch one day to talk to me about my fears. By the time the bread arrived I was nearly in tears, purging fears that I had bottled up from school. I remember telling him that I felt like I would never find a job, and that I felt like all of the work he has done with me was time wasted because I was still unemployed.

It was at that point Mike told me about this book. He informed me that he was writing a resource guide for people who are out of work and seeking employment. Mike then proceeded to tell me why he believed in the tenets of the book, and in his process of networking. It was during this meeting that I pushed back on Mike's comments and allowed my fear to get the better of me stating, "If the process worked, I would not be in the position I'm in." Instead of becoming angry or feeling disrespectful at my inability to see the big picture, Mike made me an offer.

Mike looked at me from across the table and said, "I believe in this process because I have seen it work for many people, but I understand your skepticism. I know you are scared. You don't know if you will be employed when you graduate, or worse when bills start coming in, so trust me. I want you to begin working with my company after graduation and live this book. You will be given a chance to interview people I've helped mentor along the way, as well as continue to receive coaching while working for me. I want you to do everything you can to find holes in my claims and issues with my strategies, and, if at the end of a year you remain a skeptic, well, you will have proven me wrong."

I was taken aback. I promised to test each and every claim in the book, all while continuing to build my network and follow the path set before me. As I left the meeting I drove back to school. I knew that if done right, we were about to create something special and personally rewarding. I followed the outline of the book. I met with people who walked along this path before me, and I checked every claim Mike called out. When I signed on, I sought to fill in the gaps in Mike's book with knowledge not present. What I discovered was Mike's knowledge filled in the gaps of my professional preparation.

I first heard Mike utter the words "Life is a Series of Intersections" in April 2011. He was discussing with me the importance of networking, and how at twenty-two it is impossible to know how every person you interact with will affect your future. The first time I heard the phrase I dismissed it as a lovely platitude, but not as something holding much merit. Being twenty-two the phrase didn't really make sense to me. It goes against everything the digital world I grew up in has taught me. What I would learn is meeting people is not about the here and now. It is about forming relationships and helping one another. Allow the relationship to grow. Nurture it, protect it, and look for ways to extend it. The power of this phrase comes from understanding the big picture. It comes from realizing that everyone you meet has the opportunity to be sitting on the other side of the table from you in a future interview, that you never know who is going to need your services in the days to come, and that you never know where life's journey will take you.

Understanding this concept is a paradigm shift. It is an evolution in thinking that allowed me to continue following the path set forth in this book. The notion that life is a series of intersections is what drives home the importance and power of networking and allows one to begin the true phase of self-discovery.

Building Confidence

The idea of networking terrified me when I first walked through the doors at Core Consulting. Maybe it was because of the heightened emphasis my college advisors place on it, maybe it was because secretly I am more self-conscious than gregarious, but whatever the reason, networking seemed impossible. I would attend career fairs and events while in college, but most of the time I would stand in the corner and not say much. It was early on in my journey with Core that Mike taught me two very important lessons. One, that you get something far greater out of everything you put your commitment into, so going in with a positive and confident attitude is imperative; and two, that there is more to networking than just showing up.

I took Mike's advice to heart, and slowly began to expose myself cautiously to more and more networking engagements. The first few events were extremely uncomfortable. My voice would crack as I introduced myself to people, and shook their hand with my sweaty palms. I was still scared, but because of my commitment to this process, I was forced to continue exposing myself to these events, and it got easier each time.

As I attended more and more functions, I slowly began to recognize familiar faces from previous events, and even became friends with some of the individuals. If it weren't for the research of this book, I may have never pushed myself out of my comfort zone, and I would have severely limited my opportunities for the future.

Each time I told my story my confidence grew. It was no longer a struggle for me to fight through a clouded head of anxious thoughts to remember my job title and college name. And what I found was that the more confidence I gained telling my story, the better the story began to sound. I was able to include more details, funny anecdotes, and even possible goals for the future because I had practiced telling my story so much. Networking like anything else is a skill, and when Mike claims that practice is critically important it is so true. I wanted to take some time to learn more about the way this advice has helped others, so I sat down with an individual named Brian who is now an executive for a major toy company.

When Brian began looking for his next career challenge, he asked Mike to sit down and share some advice with him. Mike told him the same advice that has been explained in this book, and Brian took it to heart. Instead of looking at only opportunities that met the filters he had established for his search, Brian opened his scope and looked for jobs that would not normally attract him, and some in which he was not even qualified. What he began to see is that each time he interviewed he told his story better and better, but that was not the only benefit.

Brian noticed that through each interview he was able to learn and discern things that were helpful in other interviews in the same industry. With each successive interview Brian claimed that he "felt that he was now an authority" on subjects he would not have known to bring up if it were not for previous interviews. Because of his willingness to expand his range and seek fresh opportunities, Brian had concurrent offers from four separate companies. Brian was in control of his own destiny because of the years of hard work he put into his resume before, but also because of his openness to new careers. Now employed, Brian claims, "I couldn't be happier. It is a perfect fit, and I never would have found it if Mike didn't encourage me to apply to positions outside of my narrowed sights."

Upon hearing Brian's story I was instantly curious if the same principles would apply to someone who didn't have as impressive a resume. Through my networking, and through speaking with friends-of-friends, I was introduced to some key people in the creative industries. After listening to Brian, I decided to reach out to these connections and see if there were ways to get interviewed and questioned at each of the organizations.

After a few weeks of trading emails I was able to get a series of interviews at a prominent, national advertising agency. Unlike every other interview I have undergone, this interview had no stakes. I was not out of work, I was not desperate for their acceptance, I was simply attempting to practice telling my story. Throughout that day I met with various recruiters and creative executives to discuss the environment, possibilities, and my experience. It is amazing how liberating it is to tell your story with no pressure. You are able to truly be yourself in the interview process, and clearly define what you have accomplished and how you did it. I was shocked at some of the articulate and poetic ways I was able to present myself, and hearing me interview like that proved that I had it in me. I would truly encourage everyone to practice telling your story and interview, because you never know what you might discover.

I left the agency that day on a cloud. I knew I wouldn't get the job, and I didn't care. I was happy doing what I was doing, but I discovered something within myself that was truly groundbreaking for me. It gave me a huge boost of confidence, and I would later use that confidence, and this practice, to help prepare me for my next opportunity.

Modern Day Cowboy

When I arrived at Core Consulting I didn't understand the comprehensive nature of the consulting business. I knew that consulting was involved in strategic planning and development, but I wasn't aware how consultants work. In order to fully understand another alternative to a corporate job, I sat down with a veteran consultant, Monty, to learn more about his history.

As I sat down to talk with Monty, his first sentence struck me as the perfect synopsis of what consulting is in a nutshell. Monty said, "Consultants are like modern day gunslingers. They're cowboys who come into an organization, walk past the HR department, and as well, the internal politics, and they walk straight up to the problem and defeat it." This analogy helped clarify for me exactly what consulting is. You are the person called in to fix the problem, and then you move on and head over to the next project in trouble.

I was curious what draws a person to consulting. Essentially I wanted to know if consultants are born or made, so I asked Monty how he got into the business. He explained, "I worked in corporate America for seven years. I had a great job at a great bank programming alongside great people, but I never felt like that was what I was meant to do. Sometimes in corporations the rules are just too tight and I hated that." I became confused upon hearing this. I didn't understand how you could enjoy something all the while hating the nucleus of it at the same time, so I decided to probe further.

Monty described his feelings saying, "I hated finding new ways to do things, finding ways that are more productive, more efficient, more intuitive, and then being told we can't implement the change because it goes against process." Through his clarification I began to understand that it takes a certain type of person with a great deal of brass to become a consultant.

It became clear to me not everyone is cut out for consulting. Some people enjoy the structure and safety of working for a corporation, having a role, and fulfilling their duties, and nothing is wrong with that. This interview helped me understand that being successful in business truly hinges on knowing yourself and applying that knowledge appropriately.

I asked Monty about this hypothesis to gain his thoughts on the subject. He agreed, stating, "Consulting is not for everyone - and realizing that is the first step to becoming a successful consultant. In order to be a successful consultant, on top of all I've said, you have to see ability within yourself that you can then market for others to buy. If you have a marketable skill that people will pay for, and you like the idea of being a gunslinger instead of full time employee, then you just have to take the leap and do it."

Putting My Knowledge to Use

In the early weeks of 2013 it became apparent that it was time for me to begin putting the knowledge I had gained through my personal journey to good use. After a phase of self-discovery, practicing and networking, and applying my own lenses and filters to the opportunities, it was time for me to begin a job hunt of my own using the principles from the book.

I began with the evaluation of my resume. I had a fine resume upon entering the workforce. I spent time in the Center of Career Planning at school, so I avoided all of the huge pitfalls. My spelling and grammar were correct, it was formatted to perfectly fit the page, it was concise, and at first glance, it looked fine. But upon closer evaluation I began to notice things that could be improved.

After all of the knowledge I had accumulated through this book, my interviews, and experiences, finding improvements to make upon my resume was not a challenge. The first thing I noticed was the need to improve my objective statement. My resume always possessed an objective statement that spoke to why I wanted a job, but it wasn't tailored to each job for which I was applying. While it was well crafted and nicely worded, it failed to mention why I wanted this position, and it read as nothing more than a pleasant introduction. The next mistake I discovered was routinely outlining my responsibilities in prior positions. Because of my diligence and hard work, I have been able to accumulate an impressive resume for someone my age, but I was doing myself a great disservice by not explaining what I achieved in each role. For example, "asked to develop plans for social media marketing," became "Researched, developed and implemented the inaugural social media marketing strategy culminating in over one thousand more eyes seeing each news update posted."

Through Mike's coaching, as well as learning from other executives, I also discovered that less is more. Instead of listing all seven tasks I managed at my previous employer, limiting that list to the four that directly translate into the job for which I'm applying helped improve my resume a great deal. Gaining the understanding that my qualifications should be judged on quality not quantity completely changed the way I formatted my resume.

After making these critical adjustments in my resume, I began to scan my network looking for opportunities. This is where all of the hours of anxious, awkward, and uncomfortable small talk truly paid off for me. Even though networking was not something I felt comfortable with, when it came time to convey my resume, I was more confident. Within my network, I knew who I could reach out to for advice, and who would be willing to introduce me to people who not only align with me professionally, but with my values and personality, as well.

I leaned on my network, and after a few preliminary meetings began to narrow my focus to a few opportunities that were the best fit. Now, I was able to send out my resume confidently to those employers, knowing the opportunity was present, and knowing I had the confidence to meet the requirements and achieve the goals expressed in the job description.

In January 2013 I had the opportunity to interview for a position that seemed like the perfect fit for me. I submitted my newly revamped resume. I included a personalized cover letter along with selected writing samples.

This brings up the first point that is essential when searching for a job: the descriptions are usually considered guidelines and not requirements. I didn't have the minimum years of experience this company posted inside their requirements, but my collective years of work (including school work) satisfied their requirements.

I submitted my resume even with my modest accomplishments, thinking I would bring my ingenuity, work ethic and total commitment to the job to quickly learn what I did not know. If it weren't for Mike's advice to not disqualify oneself too early, I may have overlooked the position all together.

Wanting to learn more about both the company and the position, I reached out to my network, albeit rather limited. From my own introspection I knew I needed continued mentoring and a strong corporate culture and value system. I was fortunate in my limited reach to gain advice, knowledge, and insight from several people who were affiliated with or knew the company. Everything I learned increased my interest with this company and heightened my appetite to know even more.

One thing I really never understood, and that Mike certainly drove home while mentoring me, is that interviewing is a two-way street. In my previous interviews, I was desperate for acceptance, wanting the offer so badly that I failed to find out if it was a good fit for me. With this job search I really took my time and didn't attempt to force anything, which I believe played a pivotal role in the process.

Within a few days I got a call from the employer stating that they wanted to bring me in for an interview. I was ecstatic. I knew that the practice I had received from my other interviews prepared me for this moment. I felt increased confidence to tell my story in the interview, that the company was indeed a great fit for me, and all that remained was being myself and providing a strong interview.

Instead of getting overly excited and forgetting to prepare, I continued to follow the framework of this book. I began by researching the company more thoroughly and learning everything that could possibly help me. I truly immersed myself in preparation a few days before the interview.

On the day of the interview I dressed 'smartly', a suit and tie, even though I knew that would be considered "overdressing" for the organization. For me, dressing up for the interview instilled greater self-confidence. One of the things that I believed separated me from any competitors was my preparation. Being able to speak in specifics about projects and the organization really does showcase your preparedness. I also made sure to speak in inclusive terms because, as Mike points out, engaging in equality and inclusion during the interview can also help distinguish you from others.

My interview consisted of everything. I was aptitude tested, drug tested, completed credit and background checks, and had multiple interviews. It was a process that extended across multiple days. To interview for one of your top-tier company positions, be prepared to run the gauntlet. There is nothing scary or intimidating about any single part, but all strung together, it can seem overwhelming. If you are well prepared, it won't likely affect you. The more you are tested, the quicker the field gets reduced. Embrace the challenge. Don't run from it. It may seem like a marathon, but the reward at the end is indescribable.

After the interview I met with a few of my prospective team members and then went on my way. They promised to call me within the next couple of days. All in all I felt great about my interviews. Regardless how things would culminate, I felt as though I responded well to this opportunity.

The very next day I received a call from the company. They informed me they wanted to make me an offer. I listened to the offer and didn't need long to determine this was the right move for me. I analyzed the offer, and happily accepted.

In sitting back afterwards and reflecting, I realized this was the culmination of months of hard work, and years of mentorship and preparation. I would be remiss to not publically thank Mike at the close of his first book. I feel incredibly blessed to have had this advantage. Mike afforded me the opportunity and helped prepare me to walk this path. I have attempted to detail how this framework helped me and how it can help others.

It is because of my journey that I have this new position. It is the best fit, with a solid, well-respected company, and comes at an opportune time in my life. Some would say it was serendipitous, others would say it was simply coincidence. For me, I believe it to be a true life intersection.

I know this framework will work for you if you will stay committed to it. I hope you enjoy your journey as much as I have my own. Good luck, old friend.

Notes

Introduction – My Why

xv. (Simon Sinek) Simon Sinek, *Start With Why*, (Portfolio Trade, reprint edition, 2011)

xv. (People don't buy what you do) Simon Sinek, *How Great Leaders Inspire Action*, TEDxPugetSound, [online]. Available from http://www.ted.com/talks/simon_sinek_how_great_leaders_inspire_action.html

xv. (Joseph Campbell) Joseph Campbell, Bill Moyers Collaborator, *The Power of Myth*, (Anchor, 1991), p.285

xv. (Jiro Ono) David Gelb, Director, *Jiro Dreams of Sushi*, DVD 2012

xvi. (Now, Discover Your Strengths) Marcus Buckingham and Donald Clifton, *Now, Discover Your Strengths*, (Free Press, 2001), p.6

The Framework

xxvii. (LeBron James) Jeff Zilligitt, *LeBron James outshines Paul George as Heat beat Pacers* (USA Today Sports, 5/23/13)

xxvii. (Sigmund Freud) Sigmund Freud, *Beyond the Pleasure Principle*, (Acheron, 2012)

Abundance and Gratitude

3. (Not Enough) Chuck Danes, *The Power of Gratitude*, (www.abundance-and-happiness.com/gratitude.html)

5. (Grateful thinking) Psychology Today, *The Benefits of Gratitude*, (Psych Basics, Gratitude) www.psychologytoday.com/asics/gratitude

7.   (George Lucas) Joseph Campbell, The Power of Myth DVD
         chapter 4, *The Mythology of Star Wars*

Personal Values

15.   (Plateaus of values) MindTools.com (2011), *What Are Your
         Values?*, [online]. Available from
         http://mindtools.com/pages/article/newTED_85.htm
         [accessed March, 8, 2013]
15.   (Plateaus of values) gurusoftware.com (2013), *Power of values to
         shape our lives,* [online]. Available from
         http://www.gurusoftware.com/GuruNet/Personal/Topics/
         Values.htm [accessed March 8, 2013]
15.   (Freudian) Gregory Mitchell, *Sigmund Freud & Freudian
         Psychoanalysis,* [online]. Available from
         http://rans4mind.com/mind-development/freud.html
         [accessed March 12, 2013]
21.   (Five Balls) James Patterson, Suzanne's Diary to Nicholas (New
         York, NY, Little, Brown, 2001), p. 20-21.

Dead-End Jobs

23.   (Karl Lagerfeld, Mellody Hobson) The Wall Street Journal, The
         Columnists topic: Discipline, [online]. Available from
         http://nline.wsj.com/article/SB100014241278873233752045782
         70200018521038.html [accessed February 14, 2013]
25-27.   (Dual-Factor Theory) Frederick Hertzberg, *Two-factor theory,*
         [online]. Available from
         http://en.wikipedia.org/wiki/Two-factor_theory [accessed
         January 11, 2013]
25.   (People leave bosses, not their jobs) Marcus Buckingham &
         Curt Coffman, *First, Break All the Rules,* (New York, NY, Simon
         & Schuster, 1999) p. 33.
25.   (Studies suggest) 2002 Watson Wyatt study, *"Strategic Rewards
         Charting the Course Forward: Maximizing the Value of Reward
         Programs," two of the five main reasons op performers eave a
         company are dissatisfaction with management and conflicts with
         supervisors.*

The Grass Isn't Always Greener

30.   (What is Happiness?) Martin E.P. Seligman, Acacia C. Parks and Tracy Steen, *a balanced psychology and a full life, 2004* (2004 The Royal Society)

30.   (The Pleasant Life) Peterson C., Park N., & Seligman, M.E.P. (2005). *Orientations to happiness and life satisfaction: The full life versus the empty life.* (Journal of Happiness Studies) p. 6, 25-41

Confidence

40.   (Gail) Carol Hazard, *Bunker sees job loss as an opportunity,* (Richmond Times-Dispatch, 1/20/13), p. D1

41.   (Dr. Albert Mehrabian)
      http://en.wikipedia.org/wiki/Albert_Mehrabian

42.   (Leadership Presence) Belle Halpern and Kathy Lubar, *Leadership Presence,* (New York, NY, Gotham 2004)

Interlude

60.   (Noel Tichy) Noel Tichy. Available from
      http://en.wikipedia.org/wiki/Noel_Tichy

60.   (Scott Harrison, Charity:Water) Meet The Founder. Available from https://www.charitywater.org/about/scotts_story.php

Networking

66.   (Matt Youngquist) Wendy Kaufman, *A Successful Job Search: It's all about Networking,* (NPR, 2011). Available from http://www.npr.org/2011/02/08/133474431/a-successful-job-search-its-all-about-networking

66.   (Right Management) Damarious Page, *The Importance of Networking in a Job Search,* (Demand Media). Available from http://work.chron.com/importance-networking-job-search-8009.html

66.   (Randall Powell) C. Randall Powell, *Career Planning Strategies: Hire Me!* , (Kendall Hunt, 5th edition 2013), *p. 427*

68.   (Adam Grant) Adam M. Grant Ph.D., *Give and Take: A Revolutionary Approach to Success,* (Viking Adult, 2013)

68. (Adam Grant) Susan Dominus, *Is Giving the Secret to Getting Ahead?* (The New York Times Magazine, 3/27/13)

Entrepreneurship

84. (Paul Reynolds & David Audretsch), *Entrepreneurship.* Available from http://en.wikipedia.org/wiki/Entrepreneurship
84. (Mike Michalowicz) Mathew Toren & Adam Toren, *Big Vision: Lessons on how to Dominate Your Market from Self-Made Entrepreneurs Who Did it Right.* (New York, NY, Wiley, 2011)
85. (Vinod Khosla) 2009 SDForum Visionary Awards. Acceptance speech.
87. (First-time entrepreneurs have only an 18% chance of succeeding) Paul Gompers, Anna Kovner, Josh Lerner and David Scharfstein, *Performance Persistence in Entrepreneurship* (Harvard Business Review, 2008)
88. (Entrepreneur story) Gladys Edmunds, *Entrepreneurial Tightrope.* Available from http://usatoday30.usatoday.com/money/smallbusiness/columnist/edmunds/story/2012-06-19/gladys-edmunds-how-entrepreneurs-should-spend-their-free-time/55698286/1
89. (Apple) *History of Apple, Inc.,* Available from http://en.wikipedia.org/wiki/History_of_Apple_Inc.
89. (Microsoft) *History of Microsoft.* Available from http://en.wikipedia.org/wiki/History_of_Apple_Inc.
89. (Air Southwest Co.) *Southwest Airlines.* Available from http://en.wikipedia.org/wiki/Southwest_Airlines
89. (HP) *Hewlett-Packard.* Available from http://en.wikipedia.org/wiki/Hewlett-Packard

Interview Coaching

113. (Unemployment) Available from http://www.examiner.com/article/more-than-12-million-remain-unemployed
113. (Unemployment) Available from http://www.bls.gov/news.release/archives/empsit_01042013.htm

114.   (Manpower) Available from
       http://press.manpower.com/press/2012/talent-shortage/

The Dreaded Interview

125.   (Selecting the doer, not the talker) Larry Bossidy & Ram
       Charan, *Execution – The Discipline of Getting Things Done,*
       (Crown Business, 2002)

Follow-up and Next Steps

128.   (Greece Olympic athlete) Kelly Whiteside, *Athlete's Olympic dis-
       missal provides tough Twitter lessons,* (USA TODAY, 7/26/2012)

On Your Mark...Run!

147.   (Gail) Carol Hazard, *Banker sees job loss as an opportunity,*
       (Richmond Times-Dispatch, 1/20/13), p. D1

Made in the USA
Middletown, DE
11 January 2016